AF530267

# The UNDERGROUND CITY or The Black Indies

Jules Verne

Pharos Books

All rights reserved. No part of this publication may be reproduced, stored in a retrieval system, or transmitted, in any form, or by any means, electronic, mechanical, photocopying, recording or otherwise, without the prior permission of the publishers.

**ISBN: 978-93-58043-44-0**
**eISBN: 978-93-58043-16-7**

**©Publisher**

**Publisher: Pharos Books (P) Ltd.**
Plot No.-63, 1st Floor, Main Mother Dairy Road
Pandav Nagar, East Delhi-110092
**Phone:** 011-40395855, +4049916623
**WhatsApp:** +91 9319228272
**E-mail:** sales@pharosbooks.in
**Website:** www.pharosbooks.in
**First Edition:** 2024

**Printed By:** Sushma Book Binding House, Okhla
Industrial Area, Phase II, New Delhi-110020

**THE UNDERGROUND CITY**
Jules Verne

# CONTENTS

# THE UNDERGROUND CITY

## CHAPTER I

## CONTRADICTORY LETTERS

To Mr. F. R. Starr, Engineer, 30 Canongate, Edinburgh.

If Mr. James Starr will come to-morrow to the Aberfoyle coal-mines, Dochart pit, Yarrow shaft, a communication of an interesting nature will be made to him.

"Mr. James Starr will be awaited for, the whole day, at the Callander station, by Harry Ford, son of the old overman Simon Ford."

"He is requested to keep this invitation secret."

Such was the letter which James Starr received by the first post, on the 3rd December, 18—, the letter bearing the Aberfoyle postmark, county of Stirling, Scotland.

The engineer's curiosity was excited to the highest pitch. It never occurred to him to doubt whether this letter might not be a hoax. For many years he had known Simon Ford, one of the former foremen of the Aberfoyle mines, of which he, James Starr, had for twenty years, been the manager, or, as he would be termed in English coal-mines, the viewer. James Starr was a strongly-constituted man, on whom his fifty-five years weighed no more heavily than if they had been forty. He belonged to an old Edinburgh family, and was one of its most distinguished members. His labors did credit to the body of engineers who are gradually devouring the carboniferous subsoil of the United Kingdom, as much at Cardiff and Newcastle, as in the southern counties of Scotland. However, it was more particularly in the depths of the mysterious mines of Aberfoyle, which border on the Alloa mines and occupy part of the county of Stirling, that the name of

Starr had acquired the greatest renown. There, the greater part of his existence had been passed. Besides this, James Starr belonged to the Scottish Antiquarian Society, of which he had been made president. He was also included amongst the most active members of the Royal Institution; and the *Edinburgh Review* frequently published clever articles signed by him. He was in fact one of those practical men to whom is due the prosperity of England. He held a high rank in the old capital of Scotland, which not only from a physical but also from a moral point of view, well deserves the name of the Northern Athens.

We know that the English have given to their vast extent of coal-mines a very significant name. They very justly call them the "Black Indies," and these Indies have contributed perhaps even more than the Eastern Indies to swell the surprising wealth of the United Kingdom.

At this period, the limit of time assigned by professional men for the exhaustion of coal-mines was far distant and there was no dread of scarcity. There were still extensive mines to be worked in the two Americas. The manufactories, appropriated to so many different uses, locomotives, steamers, gas works, &c., were not likely to fail for want of the mineral fuel; but the consumption had so increased during the last few years, that certain beds had been exhausted even to their smallest veins. Now deserted, these mines perforated the ground with their useless shafts and forsaken galleries. This was exactly the case with the pits of Aberfoyle.

Ten years before, the last butty had raised the last ton of coal from this colliery. The underground working stock, traction engines, trucks which run on rails along the galleries, subterranean tramways, frames to support the shaft, pipes—in short, all that constituted the machinery of a mine had been brought up from its depths. The exhausted mine was like the body of a huge fantastically-shaped mastodon, from which all the organs of life have been taken, and only the skeleton remains.

Nothing was left but long wooden ladders, down the Yarrow shaft—the only one which now gave access to the lower galleries of the Dochart pit. Above ground, the sheds, formerly sheltering the outside works, still marked the spot where the shaft of that pit had been sunk, it being now abandoned, as were the other pits, of which the whole constituted the mines of Aberfoyle.

It was a sad day, when for the last time the workmen quitted the mine, in which they had lived for so many years. The engineer, James Starr, had collected the hundreds of workmen which composed the active and courageous population of the mine. Overmen, brakemen, putters, wastemen, barrowmen, masons, smiths, carpenters, outside and inside laborers, women, children, and old men, all were collected in the great yard of the Dochart pit, formerly heaped with coal from the mine.

Many of these families had existed for generations in the mine of old Aberfoyle; they were now driven to seek the means of subsistence elsewhere, and they waited sadly to bid farewell to the engineer.

James Starr stood upright, at the door of the vast shed in which he had for so many years superintended the powerful machines of the shaft. Simon Ford, the foreman of the Dochart pit, then fifty-five years of age, and other managers and overseers, surrounded him. James Starr took off his hat. The miners, cap in hand, kept a profound silence. This farewell scene was of a touching character, not wanting in grandeur.

"My friends," said the engineer, "the time has come for us to separate. The Aberfoyle mines, which for so many years have united us in a common work, are now exhausted. All our researches have not led to the discovery of a new vein, and the last block of coal has just been extracted from the Dochart pit." And in confirmation of his words, James Starr pointed to a lump of coal which had been kept at the bottom of a basket.

"This piece of coal, my friends," resumed James Starr, "is like the last drop of blood which has flowed through the veins of the mine! We shall keep it, as the first fragment of coal is kept, which was extracted a hundred and fifty years ago from the bearings of Aberfoyle. Between these two pieces, how many generations of workmen have succeeded each other in our pits! Now, it is over! The last words which your engineer will address to you are a farewell. You have lived in this mine, which your hands have emptied. The work has been hard, but not without profit for you. Our great family must disperse, and it is not probable that the future will ever again unite the scattered members. But do not forget that we have lived together for a long time, and that it will be the duty of the miners of Aberfoyle to help each other. Your old masters will not forget you either. When men have worked together, they must never be stranger to each other again. We shall keep our eye on you, and wherever you go, our recommendations shall follow you. Farewell then, my friends, and may Heaven be with you!"

So saying, James Starr wrung the horny hand of the oldest miner, whose eyes were dim with tears. Then the overmen of the different pits came forward to shake hands with him, whilst the miners waved their caps, shouting, "Farewell, James Starr, our master and our friend!"

This farewell would leave a lasting remembrance in all these honest hearts. Slowly and sadly the population quitted the yard. The black soil of the roads leading to the Dochart pit resounded for the last time to the tread of miners' feet, and silence succeeded to the bustling life which had till then filled the Aberfoyle mines.

One man alone remained by James Starr. This was the overman, Simon Ford. Near him stood a boy, about fifteen years of age, who for some years already had been employed down below.

James Starr and Simon Ford knew and esteemed each other well. "Good-by, Simon," said the engineer.

"Good-by, Mr. Starr," replied the overman, "let me add, till we meet again!"

"Yes, till we meet again. Ford!" answered James Starr. "You know that I shall be always glad to see you, and talk over old times."

"I know that, Mr. Starr."

"My house in Edinburgh is always open to you."

"It's a long way off, is Edinburgh!" answered the man shaking his head. "Ay, a long way from the Dochart pit."

"A long way, Simon? Where do you mean to live?"

"Even here, Mr. Starr! We're not going to leave the mine, our good old nurse, just because her milk is dried up! My wife, my boy, and myself, we mean to remain faithful to her!"

"Good-by then, Simon," replied the engineer, whose voice, in spite of himself, betrayed some emotion.

"No, I tell you, it's *till we meet again*, Mr. Starr, and not Just 'good-by,'" returned the foreman. "Mark my words, Aberfoyle will see you again!"

The engineer did not try to dispel the man's illusion. He patted Harry's head, again wrung the father's hand, and left the mine.

All this had taken place ten years ago; but, notwithstanding the wish which the overman had expressed to see him again, during that time Starr had heard nothing of him. It was after ten years of separation that he got this letter from Simon Ford, requesting him to take without delay the road to the old Aberfoyle colliery.

A communication of an interesting nature, what could it be? Dochart pit. Yarrow shaft! What recollections of the past these names brought back to him! Yes, that was a fine time, that of work, of struggle,—the best part of the engineer's life. Starr re-read his letter. He pondered over it in all its bearings. He much regretted that just a line more had not been added by Ford. He wished he had not been quite so laconic.

Was it possible that the old foreman had discovered some new vein? No! Starr remembered with what minute care the mines had been explored before the definite cessation of the works. He had himself proceeded to the lowest soundings without finding the least trace in the soil, burrowed in every direction. They had even attempted to find coal under strata which are usually below it, such as the Devonian red sandstone, but without result. James Starr had therefore abandoned the mine with the absolute conviction that it did not contain another bit of coal.

"No," he repeated, "no! How is it possible that anything which could have escaped my researches, should be revealed to those of Simon Ford. However, the old overman must well know that such a discovery would be the one thing in the world to interest me, and this invitation, which I must keep secret, to repair to the Dochart pit!" James Starr always came back to that.

On the other hand, the engineer knew Ford to be a clever miner, peculiarly endowed with the instinct of his trade. He had not seen him since the time when the Aberfoyle colliery was abandoned, and did not know either what he was doing or where he was living, with his wife and his son. All that he now knew was, that a rendezvous had been appointed him at the Yarrow shaft, and that Harry, Simon Ford's son, was to wait for him during the whole of the next day at the Callander station.

"I shall go, I shall go!" said Starr, his excitement increasing as the time drew near.

Our worthy engineer belonged to that class of men whose brain is always on the boil, like a kettle on a hot fire. In some of these brain kettles the ideas bubble over, in others they just simmer quietly. Now on this day, James Starr's ideas were boiling fast.

But suddenly an unexpected incident occurred. This was the drop of cold water, which in a moment was to condense all the vapors of the brain. About six in the evening, by the third post, Starr's servant brought him a second letter. This letter was enclosed in a coarse envelope, and evidently directed by a hand unaccustomed to the use of a pen. James Starr tore it open. It contained only a scrap of paper, yellowed by time, and apparently torn out of an old copy book.

On this paper was written a single sentence, thus worded:

"It is useless for the engineer James Starr to trouble himself, Simon Ford's letter being now without object."

No signature.

***

# CHAPTER II

# ON THE ROAD

The course of James Starr's ideas was abruptly stopped, when he got this second letter contradicting the first.

"What does this mean?" said he to himself. He took up the torn envelope, and examined it. Like the other, it bore the Aberfoyle postmark. It had therefore come from the same part of the county of Stirling. The old miner had evidently not written it. But, no less evidently, the author of this second letter knew the overman's secret, since it expressly contradicted the invitation to the engineer to go to the Yarrow shaft.

Was it really true that the first communication was now without object? Did someone wish to prevent James Starr from troubling himself either uselessly or otherwise? Might there not be rather a malevolent intention to thwart Ford's plans?

This was the conclusion at which James Starr arrived, after mature reflection. The contradiction which existed between the two letters only wrought in him a more keen desire to visit the Dochart pit. And besides, if after all it was a hoax, it was well worth while to prove it. Starr also thought it wiser to give more credence to the first letter than to the second; that is to say, to the request of such a man as Simon Ford, rather than to the warning of his anonymous contradictor.

"Indeed," said he, "the fact of anyone endeavoring to influence my resolution, shows that Ford's communication must be of great importance. To-morrow, at the appointed time, I shall be at the rendezvous."

In the evening, Starr made his preparations for departure. As it might happen that his absence would be prolonged for some days, he wrote to Sir W. Elphiston, President of the Royal Institution, that he should be unable to be present at the next meeting of the Society. He also wrote to excuse himself from two or three engagements which he had made for the week. Then, having ordered his servant to pack a traveling bag, he went to bed, more excited than the affair perhaps warranted.

The next day, at five o'clock, James Starr jumped out of bed, dressed himself warmly, for a cold rain was falling, and left his house in the Canongate, to go to Granton Pier to catch the steamer, which in three hours would take him up the Forth as far as Stirling.

For the first time in his life, perhaps, in passing along the Canongate, he did *not turn to look at Holyrood*, the palace of the former sovereigns of Scotland. He did not notice the sentinels who stood before its gateways, dressed in the uniform of their Highland regiment, tartan kilt, plaid and sporran complete. His whole thought was to reach Callander where Harry Ford was supposedly awaiting him.

The better to understand this narrative, it will be as well to hear a few words on the origin of coal. During the geological epoch, when the terrestrial spheroid was still in course of formation, a thick atmosphere surrounded it, saturated with watery vapors, and copiously impregnated with carbonic acid. The vapors gradually condensed in diluvial rains, which fell as if they had leapt from the necks of thousands of millions of seltzer water bottles. This liquid, loaded with carbonic acid, rushed in torrents over a deep soft soil, subject to sudden or slow alterations of form, and maintained in its semi-fluid state as much by the heat of the sun as by the fires of the interior mass. The internal heat had not as yet been collected in the center of the globe. The terrestrial crust, thin and incompletely hardened, allowed it to spread through its pores. This caused a peculiar form of vegetation, such as is probably produced on the surface of the inferior planets, Venus or Mercury, which revolve nearer than our earth around the radiant sun of our system.

The soil of the continents was covered with immense forests. Carbonic acid, so suitable for the development of the vegetable kingdom, abounded. The feet of these trees were drowned in a sort of immense lagoon, kept continually full by currents of fresh and salt waters. They eagerly assimilated to themselves the carbon which they, little by little, extracted from the atmosphere, as yet unfit for the function of life, and it may be said that they were destined to store it, in the form of coal, in the very bowels of the earth.

It was the earthquake period, caused by internal convulsions, which suddenly modified the unsettled features of the terrestrial surface. Here, an intumescence which was to become a mountain, there, an abyss which was to be filled with an ocean or a sea. There, whole forests sunk through the earth's crust, below the unfixed strata, either until they found a resting-place, such as the primitive bed of granitic rock, or, settling together in a heap, they formed a solid mass.

As the waters were contained in no bed, and were spread over every part of the globe, they rushed where they liked, tearing from the scarcely-formed rocks material with which to compose schists, sandstones, and limestones. This the roving waves bore over the submerged and now peaty forests, and deposited above them the elements of rocks which were to superpose the coal strata. In course of time, periods of which include millions of years, these earths hardened in layers, and enclosed under a thick carapace of pudding-stone, schist, compact or friable sandstone, gravel and stones, the whole of the massive forests.

And what went on in this gigantic crucible, where all this vegetable matter had accumulated, sunk to various depths? A regular chemical operation, a sort of distillation. All the carbon contained in these vegetables had agglomerated, and little by little coal was forming under the double influence of enormous pressure and the high temperature maintained by the internal fires, at this time so close to it.

Thus there was one kingdom substituted for another in this slow but irresistible reaction. The vegetable was transformed into a mineral. Plants which had lived the vegetative life in all the vigor of first creation became petrified. Some of the substances enclosed in this vast herbal left their impression on the other more rapidly mineralized products, which pressed them as an hydraulic press of incalculable power would have done.

Thus also shells, zoophytes, star-fish, polypi, spirifores, even fish and lizards brought by the water, left on the yet soft coal their exact likeness, "admirably taken off."

Pressure seems to have played a considerable part in the formation of carboniferous strata. In fact, it is to its degree of power that are due the different sorts of coal, of which industry makes use. Thus in the lowest layers of the coal ground appears the anthracite, which, being almost destitute of volatile matter, contains the greatest quantity of carbon. In the higher beds are found, on the contrary, lignite and fossil wood, substances in which the quantity of carbon is infinitely less. Between these two beds, according to the degree of pressure to which they have been subjected, are found veins of graphite and rich or poor coal. It may be asserted that it is for want of sufficient pressure that beds of peaty bog have not been completely changed into coal. So then, the origin of coal mines, in whatever part of the globe they have been discovered, is this: the absorption through the terrestrial crust of the great forests of the geological period; then, the mineralization of the vegetables obtained in the course of time, under the influence of pressure and heat, and under the action of carbonic acid.

Now, at the time when the events related in this story took place, some of the most important mines of the Scottish coal beds had been exhausted by too rapid working. In the region which extends between Edinburgh and Glasgow, for a distance of ten or twelve miles, lay the Aberfoyle colliery, of which the engineer, James Starr, had so long directed the works. For ten years these mines had been abandoned. No new seams had been discovered, although the soundings had been carried to a depth of fifteen hundred or even of two thousand feet, and when James Starr had retired, it was with the full conviction that even the smallest vein had been completely exhausted.

Under these circumstances, it was plain that the discovery of a new seam of coal would be an important event. Could Simon Ford's communication relate to a fact of this nature? This question James Starr could not cease asking himself. Was he called to make conquest of another corner of these rich treasure fields? Fain would he hope it was so.

The second letter had for an instant checked his speculations on this subject, but now he thought of that letter no longer. Besides, the son of the old overman was there, waiting at the appointed rendezvous. The anonymous letter was therefore worth nothing.

The moment the engineer set foot on the platform at the end of his journey, the young man advanced towards him.

"Are you Harry Ford?" asked the engineer quickly.

"Yes, Mr. Starr."

"I should not have known you, my lad. Of course in ten years you have become a man!"

"I knew you directly, sir," replied the young miner, cap in hand. "You have not changed. You look just as you did when you bade us good-by in the Dochart pit. I haven't forgotten that day."

"Put on your cap, Harry," said the engineer. "It's pouring, and politeness needn't make you catch cold."

"Shall we take shelter anywhere, Mr. Starr?" asked young Ford.

"No, Harry. The weather is settled. It will rain all day, and I am in a hurry. Let us go on."

"I am at your orders," replied Harry.

"Tell me, Harry, is your father well?"

"Very well, Mr. Starr."

"And your mother?"

"She is well, too."

"Was it your father who wrote telling me to come to the Yarrow shaft?"

"No, it was I."

"Then did Simon Ford send me a second letter to contradict the first?" asked the engineer quickly.

"No, Mr. Starr," answered the young miner.

"Very well," said Starr, without speaking of the anonymous letter. Then, continuing, "And can you tell me what you father wants with me?"

"Mr. Starr, my father wishes to tell you himself."

"But you know what it is?"

"I do, sir."

"Well, Harry, I will not ask you more. But let us get on, for I'm anxious to see Simon Ford. By-the-bye, where does he live?"

"In the mine."

"What! In the Dochart pit?"

"Yes, Mr. Starr," replied Harry.

"Really! has your family never left the old mine since the cessation of the works?"

"Not a day, Mr. Starr. You know my father. It is there he was born, it is there he means to die!"

"I can understand that, Harry. I can understand that! His native mine! He did not like to abandon it! And are you happy there?"

"Yes, Mr. Starr," replied the young miner, "for we love one another, and we have but few wants."

"Well, Harry," said the engineer, "lead the way."

And walking rapidly through the streets of Callander, in a few minutes they had left the town behind them.

***

## CHAPTER III

## THE DOCHART PIT

Harry Ford was a fine, strapping fellow of five and twenty. His grave looks, his habitually passive expression, had from childhood been noticed among his comrades in the mine. His regular features, his deep blue eyes, his curly hair, rather chestnut than fair, the natural grace of his person, altogether made him a fine specimen of a lowlander. Accustomed from his earliest days to the work of the mine, he was strong and hardy, as well as brave and good. Guided by his father, and impelled by his own inclinations, he had early begun his education, and at an age when most lads are little more than apprentices, he had managed to make himself of some importance, a leader, in fact, among his fellows, and few are very ignorant in a country which does all it can to remove ignorance. Though, during the first years of his youth, the pick was never out of Harry's hand, nevertheless the young miner was not long in acquiring sufficient knowledge to raise him into the upper class of the miners, and he would certainly have succeeded his father as overman of the Dochart pit, if the colliery had not been abandoned.

James Starr was still a good walker, yet he could not easily have kept up with his guide, if the latter had not slackened his pace. The young man, carrying the engineer's bag, followed the left bank of the river for about a mile. Leaving its winding course, they took a road under tall, dripping trees. Wide fields lay on either side, around isolated farms. In one field a herd of hornless cows were quietly grazing; in another sheep with silky wool, like those in a child's toy sheep fold.

The Yarrow shaft was situated four miles from Callander. Whilst walking, James Starr could not but be struck with the change in the country. He had not seen it since the day when the last ton of Aberfoyle coal had been emptied into railway trucks to be sent to Glasgow. Agricultural life had now taken the place of the more stirring, active, industrial life. The contrast was all the greater because, during winter, field work is at a standstill. But formerly, at whatever season, the mining population, above and below ground, filled the scene with animation. Great wagons of coal used to be passing night and day. The rails, with their rotten sleepers, now disused, were then constantly ground by the weight of wagons. Now stony roads took the place of the old mining tramways. James Starr felt as if he was traversing a desert.

The engineer gazed about him with a saddened eye. He stopped now and then to take breath. He listened. The air was no longer filled with distant whistlings and the panting of engines. None of those black vapors which the manufacturer loves to see, hung in the horizon, mingling with the clouds. No tall cylindrical or prismatic chimney vomited out smoke, after being fed from the mine itself; no blast-pipe was puffing out its white vapor. The ground, formerly black with coal dust, had a bright look, to which James Starr's eyes were not accustomed.

When the engineer stood still, Harry Ford stopped also. The young miner waited in silence. He felt what was passing in his companion's mind, and he shared his feelings; he, a child of the mine, whose whole life had been passed in its depths.

"Yes, Harry, it is all changed," said Starr. "But at the rate we worked, of course the treasures of coal would have been exhausted some day. Do you regret that time?"

"I do regret it, Mr. Starr," answered Harry. "The work was hard, but it was interesting, as are all struggles."

"No doubt, my lad. A continuous struggle against the dangers of landslips, fires, inundations, explosions of firedamp, like claps of thunder. One had to guard against all those perils! You say well! It was a struggle, and consequently an exciting life."

"The miners of Alva have been more favored than the miners of Aberfoyle, Mr. Starr!"

"Ay, Harry, so they have," replied the engineer.

"Indeed," cried the young man, "it's a pity that all the globe was not made of coal; then there would have been enough to last millions of years!"

"No doubt there would, Harry; it must be acknowledged, however, that nature has shown more forethought by forming our sphere principally of sandstone, limestone, and granite, which fire cannot consume."

"Do you mean to say, Mr. Starr, that mankind would have ended by burning their own globe?"

"Yes! The whole of it, my lad," answered the engineer. "The earth would have passed to the last bit into the furnaces of engines, machines, steamers, gas factories; certainly, that would have been the end of our world one fine day!"

"There is no fear of that now, Mr. Starr. But yet, the mines will be exhausted, no doubt, and more rapidly than the statistics make out!"

"That will happen, Harry; and in my opinion England is very wrong in exchanging her fuel for the gold of other nations! I know well," added the engineer, "that neither hydraulics nor electricity has yet shown all they can do, and that some day these two forces will be more completely utilized. But no matter! Coal is of a very practical use, and lends itself easily to the various wants of industry. Unfortunately man cannot produce it at will. Though our external forests grow incessantly under the influence of heat and water, our subterranean forests will not be reproduced, and if they were, the globe would never be in the state necessary to make them into coal."

James Starr and his guide, whilst talking, had continued their walk at a rapid pace. An hour after leaving Callander they reached the Dochart pit.

The most indifferent person would have been touched at the appearance this deserted spot presented. It was like the skeleton of something that had formerly lived. A few wretched trees bordered a plain where the ground was hidden under the black dust of the mineral fuel, but no cinders nor even fragments of coal were to be seen. All had been carried away and consumed long ago.

They walked into the shed which covered the opening of the Yarrow shaft, whence ladders still gave access to the lower galleries of the pit. The engineer bent over the opening. Formerly from this place could be heard the powerful whistle of the air inhaled by the ventilators. It was now a silent abyss. It was like being at the mouth of some extinct volcano.

When the mine was being worked, ingenious machines were used in certain shafts of the Aberfoyle colliery, which in this respect was very well off; frames furnished with automatic lifts, working in wooden slides, oscillating ladders, called "man-engines," which, by a simple movement, permitted the miners to descend without danger.

But all these appliances had been carried away, after the cessation of the works. In the Yarrow shaft there remained only a long succession of ladders, separated at every fifty feet by narrow landings. Thirty of these ladders placed thus end to end led the visitor down into the lower gallery, a depth of fifteen hundred feet. This was the only way of communication which existed between the bottom of the Dochart pit and the open air. As to air, that came in by the Yarrow shaft, from whence galleries communicated with another shaft whose orifice opened at a higher level; the warm air naturally escaped by this species of inverted siphon.

"I will follow you, my lad," said the engineer, signing to the young man to precede him.

"As you please, Mr. Starr."

"Have you your lamp?"

"Yes, and I only wish it was still the safety lamp, which we formerly had to use!"

"Sure enough," returned James Starr, "there is no fear of fire-damp explosions now!"

Harry was provided with a simple oil lamp, the wick of which he lighted. In the mine, now empty of coal, escapes of light carburetted hydrogen could not occur. As no explosion need be feared, there was no necessity for interposing between the flame and the surrounding air that metallic screen which prevents the gas from catching fire. The Davy lamp was of no use here. But if the danger did not exist, it was because the cause of it had disappeared, and with this cause, the combustible in which formerly consisted the riches of the Dochart pit.

Harry descended the first steps of the upper ladder. Starr followed. They soon found themselves in a profound obscurity, which was only relieved by the glimmer of the lamp. The young man held it above his head, the better to light his companion. A dozen ladders were descended by the engineer and his guide, with the measured step habitual to the miner. They were all still in good condition.

James Starr examined, as well as the insufficient light would permit, the sides of the dark shaft, which were covered by a partly rotten lining of wood.

Arrived at the fifteenth landing, that is to say, half way down, they halted for a few minutes.

"Decidedly, I have not your legs, my lad," said the engineer, panting.

"You are very stout, Mr. Starr," replied Harry, "and it's something too, you see, to live all one's life in the mine."

"Right, Harry. Formerly, when I was twenty, I could have gone down all at a breath. Come, forward!"

But just as the two were about to leave the platform, a voice, as yet far distant, was heard in the depths of the shaft. It came up like a sonorous billow, swelling as it advanced, and becoming more and more distinct.

"Halloo! who comes here?" asked the engineer, stopping Harry.

"I cannot say," answered the young miner.

"Is it not your father?"

"My father, Mr. Starr? no."

"Some neighbor, then?"

"We have no neighbors in the bottom of the pit," replied Harry. "We are alone, quite alone."

"Well, we must let this intruder pass," said James Starr. "Those who are descending must yield the path to those who are ascending."

They waited. The voice broke out again with a magnificent burst, as if it had been carried through a vast speaking trumpet; and soon a few words of a Scotch song came clearly to the ears of the young miner.

"The Hundred Pipers!" cried Harry. "Well, I shall be much surprised if that comes from the lungs of any man but Jack Ryan."

"And who is this Jack Ryan?" asked James Starr.

"An old mining comrade," replied Harry. Then leaning from the platform, "Halloo! Jack!" he shouted.

"Is that you, Harry?" was the reply. "Wait a bit, I'm coming." And the song broke forth again.

In a few minutes, a tall fellow of five and twenty, with a merry face, smiling eyes, a laughing mouth, and sandy hair, appeared at the bottom of the luminous cone which was thrown from his lantern, and set foot on the landing of the fifteenth ladder. His first act was to vigorously wring the hand which Harry extended to him.

"Delighted to meet you!" he exclaimed. "If I had only known you were to be above ground to-day, I would have spared myself going down the Yarrow shaft!"

"This is Mr. James Starr," said Harry, turning his lamp towards the engineer, who was in the shadow.

"Mr. Starr!" cried Jack Ryan. "Ah, sir, I could not see. Since I left the mine, my eyes have not been accustomed to see in the dark, as they used to do."

"Ah, I remember a laddie who was always singing. That was ten years ago. It was you, no doubt?"

"Ay, Mr. Starr, but in changing my trade, I haven't changed my disposition. It's far better to laugh and sing than to cry and whine!"

"You're right there, Jack Ryan. And what do you do now, as you have left the mine?"

"I am working on the Melrose farm, forty miles from here. Ah, it's not like our Aberfoyle mines! The pick comes better to my hand than the spade or hoe. And then, in the old pit, there were vaulted roofs, to merrily echo one's songs, while up above ground!—But you are going to see old Simon, Mr. Starr?"

"Yes, Jack," answered the engineer.

"Don't let me keep you then."

"Tell me, Jack," said Harry, "what was taking you to our cottage to-day?"

"I wanted to see you, man," replied Jack, "and ask you to come to the Irvine games. You know I am the piper of the place. There will be dancing and singing."

"Thank you, Jack, but it's impossible."

"Impossible?"

"Yes; Mr. Starr's visit will last some time, and I must take him back to Callander."

"Well, Harry, it won't be for a week yet. By that time Mr. Starr's visit will be over, I should think, and there will be nothing to keep you at the cottage."

"Indeed, Harry," said James Starr, "you must profit by your friend Jack's invitation."

"Well, I accept it, Jack," said Harry. "In a week we will meet at Irvine."

"In a week, that's settled," returned Ryan. "Good-by, Harry! Your servant, Mr. Starr. I am very glad to have seen you again! I can give news of you to all my friends. No one has forgotten you, sir."

"And I have forgotten no one," said Starr.

"Thanks for all, sir," replied Jack.

"Good-by, Jack," said Harry, shaking his hand. And Jack Ryan, singing as he went, soon disappeared in the heights of the shaft, dimly lighted by his lamp.

A quarter of an hour afterwards James Starr and Harry descended the last ladder, and set foot on the lowest floor of the pit.

From the bottom of the Yarrow shaft radiated numerous empty galleries. They ran through the wall of schist and sandstone, some shored up with great, roughly-hewn beams, others lined with a thick casing of wood. In every direction embankments supplied the place of the excavated veins. Artificial pillars were made of stone from neighboring quarries, and now they supported the ground, that is to say, the double layer of tertiary and quaternary soil, which formerly rested on the seam itself. Darkness now filled the galleries, formerly lighted either by the miner's lamp or by the electric light, the use of which had been introduced in the mines.

"Will you not rest a while, Mr. Starr?" asked the young man.

"No, my lad," replied the engineer, "for I am anxious to be at your father's cottage."

"Follow me then, Mr. Starr. I will guide you, and yet I daresay you could find your way perfectly well through this dark labyrinth."

"Yes, indeed! I have the whole plan of the old pit still in my head."

Harry, followed by the engineer, and holding his lamp high the better to light their way, walked along a high gallery, like the nave of a cathedral. Their feet still struck against the wooden sleepers which used to support the rails.

They had not gone more than fifty paces, when a huge stone fell at the feet of James Starr. "Take care, Mr. Starr!" cried Harry, seizing the engineer by the arm.

"A stone, Harry! Ah! these old vaultings are no longer quite secure, of course, and—"

"Mr. Starr," said Harry Ford, "it seems to me that stone was thrown, thrown as by the hand of man!"

"Thrown!" exclaimed James Starr. "What do you mean, lad?"

"Nothing, nothing, Mr. Starr," replied Harry evasively, his anxious gaze endeavoring to pierce the darkness. "Let us go on. Take my arm, sir, and don't be afraid of making a false step."

"Here I am, Harry." And they both advanced, whilst Harry looked on every side, throwing the light of his lamp into all the corners of the gallery.

"Shall we soon be there?" asked the engineer.

"In ten minutes at most."

"Good."

"But," muttered Harry, "that was a most singular thing. It is the first time such an accident has happened to me.

"That stone falling just at the moment we were passing."

"Harry, it was a mere chance."

"Chance," replied the young man, shaking his head. "Yes, chance." He stopped and listened.

"What is the matter, Harry?" asked the engineer.

"I thought I heard someone walking behind us," replied the young miner, listening more attentively. Then he added, "No, I must have been mistaken. Lean harder on my arm, Mr. Starr. Use me like a staff."

"A good solid staff, Harry," answered James Starr. "I could not wish for a better than a fine fellow like you."

They continued in silence along the dark nave. Harry was evidently preoccupied, and frequently turned, trying to catch, either some distant noise, or remote glimmer of light.

But behind and before, all was silence and darkness.

***

## CHAPTER IV

# THE FORD FAMILY

Ten minutes afterwards, James Starr and Harry issued from the principal gallery. They were now standing in a glade, if we may use this word to designate a vast and dark excavation. The place, however, was not entirely deprived of daylight. A few rays straggled in through the opening of a deserted shaft. It was by means of this pipe that ventilation was established in the Dochart pit. Owing to its lesser density, the warm air was drawn towards the Yarrow shaft. Both air and light, therefore, penetrated in some measure into the glade.

Here Simon Ford had lived with his family ten years, in a subterranean dwelling, hollowed out in the schistous mass, where formerly stood the powerful engines which worked the mechanical traction of the Dochart pit.

Such was the habitation, "his cottage," as he called it, in which resided the old overman. As he had some means saved during a long life of toil, Ford could have afforded to live in the light of day, among trees, or in any town of the kingdom he chose, but he and his wife and son preferred remaining in the mine, where they were happy together, having the same opinions, ideas, and tastes. Yes, they were quite fond of their cottage, buried fifteen hundred feet below Scottish soil. Among other advantages, there was no fear that tax gatherers, or rent collectors would ever come to trouble its inhabitants.

At this period, Simon Ford, the former overman of the Dochart pit, bore the weight of sixty-five years well. Tall, robust, well-built, he would have been regarded as one of the most conspicuous men in the district which supplies so many fine fellows to the Highland regiments.

Simon Ford was descended from an old mining family, and his ancestors had worked the very first carboniferous seams opened in Scotland. Without discussing whether or not the Greeks and Romans made use of coal, whether the Chinese worked coal mines before the Christian era, whether the French word for coal (*houille*) is really derived from the farrier Houillos, who lived in Belgium in the twelfth century, we may affirm that the beds in Great Britain were the first ever regularly worked. So early as the eleventh century, William the Conqueror divided the produce of the Newcastle bed among his companions-in-arms. At the end of the thirteenth century, a license for the mining of "sea coal" was granted by Henry III. Lastly, towards the end of the same century, mention is made of the Scotch and Welsh beds.

It was about this time that Simon Ford's ancestors penetrated into the bowels of Caledonian earth, and lived there ever after, from father to son. They were but plain miners. They labored like convicts at the work of extracting the precious combustible. It is even believed that the coal miners, like the salt-makers of that period, were actual slaves.

However that might have been, Simon Ford was proud of belonging to this ancient family of Scotch miners. He had worked diligently in the same place where his ancestors had wielded the pick, the crowbar, and the mattock. At thirty he was overman of the Dochart pit, the most important in the Aberfoyle colliery. He was devoted to his trade. During long years he zealously performed his duty. His only grief had been to perceive the bed becoming impoverished, and to see the hour approaching when the seam would be exhausted.

It was then he devoted himself to the search for new veins in all the Aberfoyle pits, which communicated underground one with another. He had had the good luck to discover several during the last period of the working. His miner's instinct assisted him marvelously, and the engineer, James Starr, appreciated him highly. It might be said that he divined the course of seams in the depths of the coal mine as a hydroscope reveals springs in the bowels of the earth. He was *par excellence* the type of a miner whose whole existence is indissolubly connected with that of his mine. He had lived there from his birth, and now that the works were abandoned he wished to live there still. His son Harry foraged for the subterranean housekeeping; as for himself, during those ten years he had not been ten times above ground.

"Go up there! What is the good?" he would say, and refused to leave his black domain. The place was remarkably healthy, subject to an equable temperature; the old overman endured neither the heat of summer nor the cold of winter. His family enjoyed good health; what more could he desire?

But at heart he felt depressed. He missed the former animation, movement, and life in the well-worked pit. He was, however, supported by one fixed idea. "No, no! the mine is not exhausted!" he repeated.

And that man would have given serious offense who could have ventured to express before Simon Ford any doubt that old Aberfoyle would one day revive! He had never given up the hope of discovering some new bed which would restore the mine to its past splendor. Yes, he would willingly, had it been necessary, have resumed the miner's pick, and with his still stout arms vigorously attacked the rock. He went through the dark galleries, sometimes alone, sometimes with his son, examining, searching for signs of coal, only to return each day, wearied, but not in despair, to the cottage.

Madge, Simon's faithful companion, his "gude-wife," to use the Scotch term, was a tall, strong, comely woman. Madge had no wish to leave the Dochart pit any more than had her husband. She shared all his hopes and regrets. She encouraged him, she urged him on, and talked to him in a way which cheered the heart of the old overman. "Aberfoyle is only asleep," she would say. "You are right about that, Simon. This is but a rest, it is not death!"

Madge, as well as the others, was perfectly satisfied to live independent of the outer world, and was the center of the happiness enjoyed by the little family in their dark cottage.

The engineer was eagerly expected. Simon Ford was standing at his door, and as soon as Harry's lamp announced the arrival of his former viewer he advanced to meet him.

"Welcome, Mr. Starr!" he exclaimed, his voice echoing under the roof of schist. "Welcome to the old overman's cottage! Though it is buried fifteen hundred feet under the earth, our house is not the less hospitable."

"And how are you, good Simon?" asked James Starr, grasping the hand which his host held out to him.

"Very well, Mr. Starr. How could I be otherwise here, sheltered from the inclemencies of the weather? Your ladies who go to Newhaven or Portobello in the summer time would do much better to pass a few months in the coal mine of Aberfoyle! They would run no risk here of catching a heavy cold, as they do in the damp streets of the old capital."

"I'm not the man to contradict you, Simon," answered James Starr, glad to find the old man just as he used to be. "Indeed, I wonder why I do not change my home in the Canongate for a cottage near you."

"And why not, Mr. Starr? I know one of your old miners who would be truly pleased to have only a partition wall between you and him."

"And how is Madge?" asked the engineer.

"The goodwife is in better health than I am, if that's possible," replied Ford, "and it will be a pleasure to her to see you at her table. I think she will surpass herself to do you honor."

"We shall see that, Simon, we shall see that!" said the engineer, to whom the announcement of a good breakfast could not be indifferent, after his long walk.

"Are you hungry, Mr. Starr?"

"Ravenously hungry. My journey has given me an appetite. I came through horrible weather."

"Ah, it is raining up there," responded Simon Ford.

"Yes, Simon, and the waters of the Forth are as rough as the sea."

"Well, Mr. Starr, here it never rains. But I needn't describe to you all the advantages, which you know as well as myself. Here we are at the cottage. That is the chief thing, and I again say you are welcome, sir."

Simon Ford, followed by Harry, ushered their guest into the dwelling. James Starr found himself in a large room lighted by numerous lamps, one hanging from the colored beams of the roof.

"The soup is ready, wife," said Ford, "and it mustn't be kept waiting any more than Mr. Starr. He is as hungry as a miner, and he shall see that our boy doesn't let us want for anything in the cottage! By-the-bye, Harry," added the old overman, turning to his son, "Jack Ryan came here to see you."

"I know, father. We met him in the Yarrow shaft."

"He's an honest and a merry fellow," said Ford; "but he seems to be quite happy above ground. He hasn't the true miner's blood in his veins. Sit down, Mr. Starr, and have a good dinner, for we may not sup till late."

As the engineer and his hosts were taking their places:

"One moment, Simon," said James Starr. "Do you want me to eat with a good appetite?"

"It will be doing us all possible honor, Mr. Starr," answered Ford.

"Well, in order to eat heartily, I must not be at all anxious. Now I have two questions to put to you."

"Go on, sir."

"Your letter told me of a communication which was to be of an interesting nature."

"It is very interesting indeed."

"To you?"

"To you and to me, Mr. Starr. But I do not want to tell it you until after dinner, and on the very spot itself. Without that you would not believe me."

"Simon," resumed the engineer, "look me straight in the face. An interesting communication? Yes. Good! I will not ask more," he added, as if he had read the reply in the old overman's eyes.

"And the second question?" asked the latter.

"Do you know, Simon, who the person is who can have written this?" answered the engineer, handing him the anonymous letter.

Ford took the letter and read it attentively. Then giving it to his son, "Do you know the writing?" he asked.

"No, father," replied Harry.

"And had this letter the Aberfoyle postmark?" inquired Simon Ford.

"Yes, like yours," replied James Starr.

"What do you think of that, Harry?" said his father, his brow darkening.

"I think, father," returned Harry, "that someone has had some interest in trying to prevent Mr. Starr from coming to the place where you invited him."

"But who," exclaimed the old miner, "who could have possibly guessed enough of my secret?" And Simon fell into a reverie, from which he was aroused by his wife.

"Let us begin, Mr. Starr," she said. "The soup is already getting cold. Don't think any more of that letter just now."

On the old woman's invitation, each drew in his chair, James Starr opposite to Madge—to do him honor—the father and son opposite to each other. It was a good Scotch dinner. First they ate "hotchpotch," soup with the meat swimming in capital broth. As old Simon said, his wife knew no rival in the art of preparing hotchpotch. It was the same with the "cockyleeky," a cock stewed with leeks, which merited high praise. The whole was washed down with excellent ale, obtained from the best brewery in Edinburgh.

But the principal dish consisted of a "haggis," the national pudding, made of meat and barley meal. This remarkable dish, which inspired the poet Burns with one of his best odes, shared the fate of all the good things in this world—it passed away like a dream.

Madge received the sincere compliments of her guest. The dinner ended with cheese and oatcake, accompanied by a few small glasses of "usquebaugh," capital whisky, five and twenty years old—just Harry's age. The repast lasted a good hour. James Starr and Simon Ford had not only eaten much, but talked much too, chiefly of their past life in the old Aberfoyle mine.

Harry had been rather silent. Twice he had left the table, and even the house. He evidently felt uneasy since the incident of the stone, and wished to examine the environs of the cottage. The anonymous letter had not contributed to reassure him.

Whilst he was absent, the engineer observed to Ford and his wife, "That's a fine lad you have there, my friends."

"Yes, Mr. Starr, he is a good and affectionate son," replied the old overman earnestly.

"Is he happy with you in the cottage?"

"He would not wish to leave us."

"Don't you think of finding him a wife, some day?"

"A wife for Harry," exclaimed Ford. "And who would it be? A girl from up yonder, who would love merry-makings and dancing, who would prefer her clan to our mine! Harry wouldn't do it!"

"Simon," said Madge, "you would not forbid that Harry should take a wife."

"I would forbid nothing," returned the old miner, "but there's no hurry about that. Who knows but we may find one for him—"

Harry re-entered at that moment, and Simon Ford was silent.

When Madge rose from the table, all followed her example, and seated themselves at the door of the cottage. "Well, Simon," said the engineer, "I am ready to hear you."

"Mr. Starr," responded Ford, "I do not need your ears, but your legs. Are you quite rested?"

"Quite rested and quite refreshed, Simon. I am ready to go with you wherever you like."

"Harry," said Simon Ford, turning to his son, "light our safety lamps."

"Are you going to take safety lamps!" exclaimed James Starr, in amazement, knowing that there was no fear of explosions of fire-damp in a pit quite empty of coal.

"Yes, Mr. Starr, it will be prudent."

"My good Simon, won't you propose next to put me in a miner's dress?"

"Not just yet, sir, not just yet!" returned the old overman, his deep-set eyes gleaming strangely.

Harry soon reappeared, carrying three safety lamps. He handed one of these to the engineer, the other to his father, and kept the third hanging from his left hand, whilst his right was armed with a long stick.

"Forward!" said Simon Ford, taking up a strong pick, which was leaning against the wall of the cottage.

"Forward!" echoed the engineer. "Good-by, Madge."

"*God* speed you!" responded the good woman.

"A good supper, wife, do you hear?" exclaimed Ford. "We shall be hungry when we come back, and will do it justice!"

***

## CHAPTER V

## SOME STRANGE PHENOMENA

Many superstitious beliefs exist both in the Highlands and Lowlands of Scotland. Of course the mining population must furnish its contingent of legends and fables to this mythological repertory. If the fields are peopled with imaginary beings, either good or bad, with much more reason must the dark mines be haunted to their lowest depths. Who shakes the seam during tempestuous nights? who puts the miners on the track of an as yet unworked vein? who lights the fire-damp, and presides over the terrible explosions? who but some spirit of the mine? This, at least, was the opinion commonly spread among the superstitious Scotch.

In the first rank of the believers in the supernatural in the Dochart pit figured Jack Ryan, Harry's friend. He was the great partisan of all these superstitions. All these wild stories were turned by him into songs, which earned him great applause in the winter evenings.

But Jack Ryan was not alone in his belief. His comrades affirmed, no less strongly, that the Aberfoyle pits were haunted, and that certain strange beings were seen there frequently, just as in the Highlands. To hear them talk, it would have been more extraordinary if nothing of the kind appeared. Could there indeed be a better place than a dark and deep coal mine for the freaks of fairies, elves, goblins, and other actors in the fantastical dramas? The scenery was all ready, why should not the supernatural personages come there to play their parts?

So reasoned Jack Ryan and his comrades in the Aberfoyle mines. We have said that the different pits communicated with each other by means of long subterranean galleries. Thus there existed beneath the county of Stirling a vast tract, full of burrows, tunnels, bored with caves, and perforated with shafts, a subterranean labyrinth, which might be compared to an enormous ant-hill.

Miners, though belonging to different pits, often met, when going to or returning from their work. Consequently there was a constant opportunity of exchanging talk, and circulating the stories which had their origin in the mine, from one pit to another. These accounts were transmitted with marvelous rapidity, passing from mouth to mouth, and gaining in wonder as they went.

Two men, however, better educated and with more practical minds than the rest, had always resisted this temptation. They in no degree believed in the intervention of spirits, elves, or goblins. These two were Simon Ford and his son. And they proved it by continuing to inhabit the dismal crypt, after the desertion of the Dochart pit. Perhaps good Madge, like every Highland woman, had some leaning towards the supernatural. But she had to repeat all these stories to herself, and so she did, most conscientiously, so as not to let the old traditions be lost.

Even had Simon and Harry Ford been as credulous as their companions, they would not have abandoned the mine to the imps and fairies. For ten years, without missing a single day, obstinate and immovable in their convictions, the father and son took their picks, their sticks, and their lamps. They went about searching, sounding the rock with a sharp blow, listening if it would return a favor-able sound. So long as the soundings had not been pushed to the granite of the primary formation, the Fords were agreed that the search, unsuccessful to-day, might succeed to-morrow, and that it ought to be resumed. They spent their whole life in endeavoring to bring Aberfoyle back to its former prosperity. If the father died before the hour of success, the son was to go on with the task alone.

It was during these excursions that Harry was more particularly struck by certain phenomena, which he vainly sought to explain. Several times, while walking along some narrow cross-alley, he seemed to hear sounds similar to those which would be produced by violent blows of a pickax against the wall.

Harry hastened to seek the cause of this mysterious work. The tunnel was empty. The light from the young miner's lamp, thrown on the wall, revealed no trace of any recent work with pick or crowbar. Harry would then ask himself if it was not the effect of some acoustic illusion, or some strange and fantastic echo. At other times, on suddenly throwing a bright light into a suspicious-looking cleft in the rock, he thought he saw a shadow. He rushed forward. Nothing, and there was no opening to permit a human being to evade his pursuit!

Twice in one month, Harry, whilst visiting the west end of the pit, distinctly heard distant reports, as if some miner had exploded a charge of dynamite. The second time, after many careful researches, he found that a pillar had just been blown up.

By the light of his lamp, Harry carefully examined the place attacked by the explosion. It had not been made in a simple embankment of stones, but in a mass of schist, which had penetrated to this depth in the coal stratum. Had the object of the explosion been to discover a new vein? Or had someone wished simply to destroy this portion of the mine? Thus he questioned, and when he made known this occurrence to his father, neither could the old overman nor he himself answer the question in a satisfactory way.

"It is very queer," Harry often repeated. "The presence of an unknown being in the mine seems impossible, and yet there can be no doubt about it. Does someone besides ourselves wish to find out if a seam yet exists? Or, rather, has he attempted to destroy what remains of the Aberfoyle mines? But for what reason? I will find that out, if it should cost me my life!"

A fortnight before the day on which Harry Ford guided the engineer through the labyrinth of the Dochart pit, he had been on the point of attaining the object of his search. He was going over the southwest end of the mine, with a large lantern in his hand. All at once, it seemed to him that a light was suddenly extinguished, some hundred feet before him, at the end of a narrow passage cut obliquely through the rock. He darted forward.

His search was in vain. As Harry would not admit a supernatural explanation for a physical occurrence, he concluded that certainly some strange being prowled about in the pit. But whatever he could do, searching with the greatest care, scrutinizing every crevice in the gallery, he found nothing for his trouble.

If Jack Ryan and the other superstitious fellows in the mine had seen these lights, they would, without fail, have called them supernatural, but Harry did not dream of doing so, nor did his father. And when they talked over these phenomena, evidently due to a physical cause, "My lad," the old man would say, "we must wait. It will all be explained some day."

However, it must be observed that, hitherto, neither Harry nor his father had ever been exposed to any act of violence. If the stone which had fallen at the feet of James Starr had been thrown by the hand of some ill-disposed person, it was the first criminal act of that description.

James Starr was of opinion that the stone had become detached from the roof of the gallery; but Harry would not admit of such a simple explanation. According to him, the stone had not fallen, it had been thrown; for otherwise, without rebounding, it could never have described a trajectory as it did.

Harry saw in it a direct attempt against himself and his father, or even against the engineer.

***

## CHAPTER VI

## SIMON FORD'S EXPERIMENT

The old clock in the cottage struck one as James Starr and his two companions went out. A dim light penetrated through the ventilating shaft into the glade. Harry's lamp was not necessary here, but it would very soon be of use, for the old overman was about to conduct the engineer to the very end of the Dochart pit.

After following the principal gallery for a distance of two miles, the three explorers—for, as will be seen, this was a regular exploration—arrived at the entrance of a narrow tunnel. It was like a nave, the roof of which rested on woodwork, covered with white moss. It followed very nearly the line traced by the course of the river Forth, fifteen hundred feet above.

"So we are going to the end of the last vein?" said James Starr.

"Ay! You know the mine well still."

"Well, Simon," returned the engineer, "it will be difficult to go further than that, if I don't mistake."

"Yes, indeed, Mr. Starr. That was where our picks tore out the last bit of coal in the seam. I remember it as if it were yesterday. I myself gave that last blow, and it re-echoed in my heart more dismally than on the rock. Only sandstone and schist were round us after that, and when the truck rolled towards the shaft, I followed, with my heart as full as though it were a funeral. It seemed to me that the soul of the mine was going with it."

The gravity with which the old man uttered these words impressed the engineer, who was not far from sharing his sentiments. They were those of the sailor who leaves his disabled vessel—of the proprietor who sees the house of his ancestors pulled down. He pressed Ford's hand; but now the latter seized that of the engineer, and, wringing it:

"That day we were all of us mistaken," he exclaimed. "No! The old mine was not dead. It was not a corpse that the miners abandoned; and I dare to assert, Mr. Starr, that its heart beats still."

"Speak, Ford! Have you discovered a new vein?" cried the engineer, unable to contain himself. "I know you have! Your letter could mean nothing else."

"Mr. Starr," said Simon Ford, "I did not wish to tell any man but yourself."

"And you did quite right, Ford. But tell me how, by what signs, are you sure?"

"Listen, sir!" resumed Simon. "It is not a seam that I have found."

"What is it, then?"

"Only positive proof that such a seam exists."

"And the proof?"

"Could fire-damp issue from the bowels of the earth if coal was not there to produce it?"

"No, certainly not!" replied the engineer. "No coal, no fire-damp. No effects without a cause."

"Just as no smoke without fire."

"And have you recognized the presence of light carburetted hydrogen?"

"An old miner could not be deceived," answered Ford. "I have met with our old enemy, the fire-damp!"

"But suppose it was another gas," said Starr. "Firedamp is almost without smell, and colorless. It only really betrays its presence by an explosion."

"Mr. Starr," said Simon Ford, "will you let me tell you what I have done? Harry had once or twice observed something remarkable in his excursions to the west end of the mine. Fire, which suddenly went out, sometimes appeared along the face of the rock or on the embankment of the further galleries. How those flames were lighted, I could not and cannot say. But they were evidently owing to the presence of fire-damp, and to me fire-damp means a vein of coal."

"Did not these fires cause any explosion?" asked the engineer quickly.

"Yes, little partial explosions," replied Ford, "such as I used to cause myself when I wished to ascertain the presence of fire-damp. Do you remember how formerly it was the custom to try to prevent explosions before our good genius, Humphry Davy, invented his safety-lamp?"

"Yes," replied James Starr. "You mean what the 'monk,' as the men called him, used to do. But I have never seen him in the exercise of his duty."

"Indeed, Mr. Starr, you are too young, in spite of your five-and-fifty years, to have seen that. But I, ten years older, often saw the last 'monk' working in the mine. He was called so because he wore a long robe like a monk. His proper name was the 'fireman.' At that time there was no other means of destroying the bad gas but by dispersing it in little explosions, before its buoyancy had collected it in too great quantities in the heights of the galleries. The monk, as we called him, with his face masked, his head muffled up, all his body tightly wrapped in a thick felt cloak, crawled along the ground. He could breathe down there, when the air was pure; and with his right hand he waved above his head a blazing torch. When the firedamp had accumulated in the air, so as to form a detonating mixture, the explosion occurred without being fatal, and, by often renewing this operation, catastrophes were prevented. Sometimes the 'monk' was injured or killed in his work, then another took his place. This was done in all mines until the Davy lamp was universally adopted. But I knew the plan, and by its means I discovered the presence of firedamp and consequently that of a new seam of coal in the Dochart pit."

All that the old overman had related of the so-called "monk" or "fireman" was perfectly true. The air in the galleries of mines was formerly always purified in the way described.

Fire-damp, marsh-gas, or carburetted hydrogen, is colorless, almost scentless; it burns with a blue flame, and makes respiration impossible. The miner could not live in a place filled with this injurious gas, any more than one could live in a gasometer full of common gas. Moreover, fire-damp, as well as the latter, a mixture of inflammable gases, forms a detonating mixture as soon as the air unites with it in a proportion of eight, and perhaps even five to the hundred. When this mixture is lighted by any cause, there is an explosion, almost always followed by a frightful catastrophe.

As they walked on, Simon Ford told the engineer all that he had done to attain his object; how he was sure that the escape of fire-damp took place at the very end of the farthest gallery in its western part, because he had provoked small and partial explosions, or rather little flames, enough to show the nature of the gas, which escaped in a small jet, but with a continuous flow.

An hour after leaving the cottage, James Starr and his two companions had gone a distance of four miles. The engineer, urged by anxiety and hope, walked on without noticing the length of the way. He pondered over all that the old miner had told him, and mentally weighed all the arguments which the latter had given in support of his belief. He agreed with him in thinking that the continued emission of carburetted hydrogen certainly showed the existence of a new coal-seam. If it had been merely a sort of pocket, full of gas, as it is sometimes found amongst the rock, it would soon have been empty, and the phenomenon have ceased. But far from that. According to Simon Ford, the fire-damp escaped incessantly, and from that fact the existence of an important vein might be considered certain. Consequently, the riches of the Dochart pit were not entirely exhausted. The chief question now was, whether this was merely a vein which would yield comparatively little, or a bed occupying a large extent.

Harry, who preceded his father and the engineer, stopped.

"Here we are!" exclaimed the old miner. "At last, thank Heaven! you are here, Mr. Starr, and we shall soon know." The old overman's voice trembled slightly.

"Be calm, my man!" said the engineer. "I am as excited as you are, but we must not lose time."

The gallery at this end of the pit widened into a sort of dark cave. No shaft had been pierced in this part, and the gallery, bored into the bowels of the earth, had no direct communication with the surface of the earth.

James Starr, with intense interest, examined the place in which they were standing. On the walls of the cavern the marks of the pick could still be seen, and even holes in which the rock had been blasted, near the termination of the working. The schist was excessively hard, and it had not been necessary to bank up the end of the tunnel where the works had come to an end. There the vein had failed, between the schist and the tertiary sandstone. From this very place had been extracted the last piece of coal from the Dochart pit.

"We must attack the dyke," said Ford, raising his pick; "for at the other side of the break, at more or less depth, we shall assuredly find the vein, the existence of which I assert."

"And was it on the surface of these rocks that you found out the fire-damp?" asked James Starr.

"Just there, sir," returned Ford, "and I was able to light it only by bringing my lamp near to the cracks in the rock. Harry has done it as well as I."

"At what height?" asked Starr.

"Ten feet from the ground," replied Harry.

James Starr had seated himself on a rock. After critically inhaling the air of the cavern, he gazed at the two miners, almost as if doubting their words, decided as they were. In fact, carburetted hydrogen is not completely scentless, and the engineer, whose sense of smell was very keen, was astonished that it had not revealed the presence of the explosive gas. At any rate, if the gas had mingled at all with the surrounding air, it could only be in a very small stream. There was no danger of an explosion, and they might without fear open the safety lamp to try the experiment, just as the old miner had done before.

What troubled James Starr was, not lest too much gas mingled with the air, but lest there should be little or none.

"Could they have been mistaken?" he murmured. "No: these men know what they are about. And yet—"

He waited, not without some anxiety, until Simon Ford's phenomenon should have taken place. But just then it seemed that Harry, like himself, had remarked the absence of the characteristic odor of fire-damp; for he exclaimed in an altered voice, "Father, I should say the gas was no longer escaping through the cracks!"

"No longer!" cried the old miner—and, pressing his lips tight together, he snuffed the air several times.

Then, all at once, with a sudden movement, "Hand me your lamp, Harry," he said.

Ford took the lamp with a trembling hand. He drew off the wire gauze case which surrounded the wick, and the flame burned in the open air.

As they had expected, there was no explosion, but, what was more serious, there was not even the slight crackling which indicates the presence of a small quantity of firedamp. Simon took the stick which Harry was holding, fixed his lamp to the end of it, and raised it high above his head, up to where the gas, by reason of its buoyancy, would naturally accumulate. The flame of the lamp, burning straight and clear, revealed no trace of the carburetted hydrogen.

"Close to the wall," said the engineer.

"Yes," responded Ford, carrying the lamp to that part of the wall at which he and his son had, the evening before, proved the escape of gas.

The old miner's arm trembled whilst he tried to hoist the lamp up. "Take my place, Harry," said he.

Harry took the stick, and successively presented the lamp to the different fissures in the rock; but he shook his head, for of that slight crackling peculiar to escaping fire-damp he heard nothing. There was no flame. Evidently not a particle of gas was escaping through the rock.

"Nothing!" cried Ford, clenching his fist with a gesture rather of anger than disappointment.

A cry escaped Harry.

"What's the matter?" asked Starr quickly.

"Someone has stopped up the cracks in the schist!"

"Is that true?" exclaimed the old miner.

"Look, father!" Harry was not mistaken. The obstruction of the fissures was clearly visible by the light of the lamp. It had been recently done with lime, leaving on the rock a long whitish mark, badly concealed with coal dust.

"It's he!" exclaimed Harry. "It can only be he!"

"He?" repeated James Starr in amazement.

"Yes!" returned the young man, "that mysterious being who haunts our domain, for whom I have watched a hundred times without being able to get at him—the author, we may now be certain, of that letter which was intended to hinder you from coming to see my father, Mr. Starr, and who finally threw that stone at us in the gallery of the Yarrow shaft! Ah! there's no doubt about it; there is a man's hand in all that!"

Harry spoke with such energy that conviction came instantly and fully to the engineer's mind. As to the old overman, he was already convinced. Besides, there they were in the presence of an undeniable fact—the stopping-up of cracks through which gas had escaped freely the night before.

"Take your pick, Harry," cried Ford; "mount on my shoulders, my lad! I am still strong enough to bear you!" The young man understood in an instant. His father propped himself up against the rock. Harry got upon his shoulders, so that with his pick he could reach the line of the fissure. Then with quick sharp blows he attacked it. Almost directly afterwards a slight sound was heard, like champagne escaping from a bottle—a sound commonly expressed by the word "puff."

Harry again seized his lamp, and held it to the opening. There was a slight report; and a little red flame, rather blue at its outline, flickered over the rock like a Will-o'-the-Wisp.

Harry leaped to the ground, and the old overman, unable to contain his joy, grasped the engineer's hands, exclaiming, "Hurrah! hurrah! hurrah! Mr. Starr. The fire-damp burns! the vein is there!"

***

# CHAPTER VII

# NEW ABERFOYLE

The old overman's experiment had succeeded. Firedamp, it is well known, is only generated in coal seams; therefore the existence of a vein of precious combustible could no longer be doubted. As to its size and quality, that must be determined later.

"Yes," thought James Starr, "behind that wall lies a carboniferous bed, undiscovered by our soundings. It is vexatious that all the apparatus of the mine, deserted for ten years, must be set up anew. Never mind. We have found the vein which was thought to be exhausted, and this time it shall be worked to the end!"

"Well, Mr. Starr," asked Ford, "what do you think of our discovery? Was I wrong to trouble you? Are you sorry to have paid this visit to the Dochart pit?"

"No, no, my old friend!" answered Starr. "We have not lost our time; but we shall be losing it now, if we do not return immediately to the cottage. To-morrow we will come back here. We will blast this wall with dynamite. We will lay open the new vein, and after a series of soundings, if the seam appears to be large, I will form a new Aberfoyle Company, to the great satisfaction of the old shareholders. Before three months have passed, the first corves full of coal will have been taken from the new vein."

"Well said, sir!" cried Simon Ford. "The old mine will grow young again, like a widow who remarries! The bustle of the old days will soon begin with the blows of the pick, and mattock, blasts of powder, rumbling of wagons, neighing of horses, creaking of machines! I shall see it all again! I hope, Mr. Starr, that you will not think me too old to resume my duties of overman?"

"No, Simon, no indeed! You wear better than I do, my old friend!"

"And, sir, you shall be our viewer again. May the new working last for many years, and pray Heaven I shall have the consolation of dying without seeing the end of it!"

The old miner was overflowing with joy. James Starr fully entered into it; but he let Ford rave for them both. Harry alone remained thoughtful. To his memory recurred the succession of singular, inexplicable circumstances attending the discovery of the new bed. It made him uneasy about the future.

An hour afterwards, James Starr and his two companions were back in the cottage. The engineer supped with good appetite, listening with satisfaction to all the plans unfolded by the old overman; and had it not been for his excitement about the next day's work, he would never have slept better than in the perfect stillness of the cottage.

The following day, after a substantial breakfast, James Starr, Simon Ford, Harry, and even Madge herself, took the road already traversed the day before. All looked like regular miners. They carried different tools, and some dynamite with which to blast the rock. Harry, besides a large lantern, took a safety lamp, which would burn for twelve hours. It was more than was necessary for the journey there and back, including the time for the working—supposing a working was possible.

"To work! to work!" shouted Ford, when the party reached the further end of the passage; and he grasped a heavy crowbar and brandished it.

"Stop one instant," said Starr. "Let us see if any change has taken place, and if the fire-damp still escapes through the crevices."

"You are right, Mr. Starr," said Harry. "Whoever stopped it up yesterday may have done it again to-day!"

Madge, seated on a rock, carefully observed the excavation, and the wall which was to be blasted.

It was found that everything was just as they left it. The crevices had undergone no alteration; the carburetted hydrogen still filtered through, though in a small stream, which was no doubt because it had had a free passage since the day before. As the quantity was so small, it could not have formed an explosive mixture with the air inside. James Starr and his companions could therefore proceed in security. Besides, the air grew purer by rising to the heights of the Dochart pit; and the fire-damp, spreading through the atmosphere, would not be strong enough to make any explosion.

"To work, then!" repeated Ford; and soon the rock flew in splinters under his skillful blows. The break was chiefly composed of pudding-stone, interspersed with sandstone and schist, such as is most often met with between the coal veins. James Starr picked up some of the pieces, and examined them carefully, hoping to discover some trace of coal.

Starr having chosen the place where the holes were to be drilled, they were rapidly bored by Harry. Some cartridges of dynamite were put into them. As soon as the long, tarred safety match was laid, it was lighted on a level with the ground. James Starr and his companions then went off to some distance.

"Oh! Mr. Starr," said Simon Ford, a prey to agitation, which he did not attempt to conceal, "never, no, never has my old heart beaten so quick before! I am longing to get at the vein!"

"Patience, Simon!" responded the engineer. "You don't mean to say that you think you are going to find a passage all ready open behind that dyke?"

"Excuse me, sir," answered the old overman; "but of course I think so! If there was good luck in the way Harry and I discovered this place, why shouldn't the good luck go on?"

As he spoke, came the explosion. A sound as of thunder rolled through the labyrinth of subterranean galleries. Starr, Madge, Harry, and Simon Ford hastened towards the spot.

"Mr. Starr! Mr. Starr!" shouted the overman. "Look! the door is broken open!"

Ford's comparison was justified by the appearance of an excavation, the depth of which could not be calculated. Harry was about to spring through the opening; but the engineer, though excessively surprised to find this cavity, held him back. "Allow time for the air in there to get pure," said he.

"Yes! beware of the foul air!" said Simon.

A quarter of an hour was passed in anxious waiting. The lantern was then fastened to the end of a stick, and introduced into the cave, where it continued to burn with unaltered brilliancy. "Now then, Harry, go," said Starr, "and we will follow you."

The opening made by the dynamite was sufficiently large to allow a man to pass through. Harry, lamp in hand, entered unhesitatingly, and disappeared in the darkness. His father, mother, and James Starr waited in silence. A minute—which seemed to them much longer—passed. Harry did not reappear, did not call. Gazing into the opening, James Starr could not even see the light of his lamp, which ought to have illuminated the dark cavern.

Had the ground suddenly given way under Harry's feet? Had the young miner fallen into some crevice? Could his voice no longer reach his companions?

The old overman, dead to their remonstrances, was about to enter the opening, when a light appeared, dim at first, but gradually growing brighter, and Harry's voice was heard shouting, "Come, Mr. Starr! come, father! The road to New Aberfoyle is open!"

If, by some superhuman power, engineers could have raised in a block, a thousand feet thick, all that portion of the terrestrial crust which supports the lakes, rivers, gulfs, and territories of the counties of Stirling, Dumbarton, and Renfrew, they would have found, under that enormous lid, an immense excavation, to which but one other in the world can be compared—the celebrated Mammoth caves of Kentucky. This excavation was composed of several hundred divisions of all sizes and shapes. It might be called a hive with numberless ranges of cells, capriciously arranged, but a hive on a vast scale, and which, instead of bees, might have lodged all the ichthyosauri, megatheriums, and pterodactyles of the geological epoch.

A labyrinth of galleries, some higher than the most lofty cathedrals, others like cloisters, narrow and winding—these following a horizontal line, those on an incline or running obliquely in all directions—connected the caverns and allowed free communication between them.

The pillars sustaining the vaulted roofs, whose curves allowed of every style, the massive walls between the passages, the naves themselves in this layer of secondary formation, were composed of sandstone and schistous rocks. But tightly packed between these useless strata ran valuable veins of coal, as if the black blood of this strange mine had circulated through their tangled network. These fields extended forty miles north and south, and stretched even under the Caledonian Canal. The importance of this bed could not be calculated until after soundings, but it would certainly surpass those of Cardiff and Newcastle.

We may add that the working of this mine would be singularly facilitated by the fantastic dispositions of the secondary earths; for by an unaccountable retreat of the mineral matter at the geological epoch, when the mass was solidifying, nature had already multiplied the galleries and tunnels of New Aberfoyle.

Yes, nature alone! It might at first have been supposed that some works abandoned for centuries had been discovered afresh. Nothing of the sort. No one would have deserted such riches. Human termites had never gnawed away this part of the Scottish subsoil; nature herself had done it all. But, we repeat, it could be compared to nothing but the celebrated Mammoth caves, which, in an extent of more than twenty miles, contain two hundred and twenty-six avenues, eleven lakes, seven rivers, eight cataracts, thirty-two unfathomable wells, and fifty-seven domes, some of which are more than four hundred and fifty feet in height. Like these caves, New Aberfoyle was not the work of men, but the work of the Creator.

Such was this new domain, of matchless wealth, the discovery of which belonged entirely to the old overman. Ten years' sojourn in the deserted mine, an uncommon pertinacity in research, perfect faith, sustained by a marvelous mining instinct—all these qualities together led him to succeed where so many others had failed. Why had the soundings made under the direction of James Starr during the last years of the working stopped just at that limit, on the very frontier of the new mine? That was all chance, which takes great part in researches of this kind.

However that might be, there was, under the Scottish subsoil, what might be called a subterranean county, which, to be habitable, needed only the rays of the sun, or, for want of that, the light of a special planet.

Water had collected in various hollows, forming vast ponds, or rather lakes larger than Loch Katrine, lying just above them. Of course the waters of these lakes had no movement of currents or tides; no old castle was reflected there; no birch or oak trees waved on their banks. And yet these deep lakes, whose mirror-like surface was never ruffled by a breeze, would not be without charm by the light of some electric star, and, connected by a string of canals, would well complete the geography of this strange domain.

Although unfit for any vegetable production, the place could be inhabited by a whole population. And who knows but that in this steady temperature, in the depths of the mines of Aberfoyle, as well as in those of Newcastle, Alloa, or Cardiff—when their contents shall have been exhausted—who knows but that the poorer classes of Great Britain will some day find a refuge?

***

## CHAPTER VIII

## EXPLORING

At Harry's call, James Starr, Madge, and Simon Ford entered through the narrow orifice which put the Dochart pit in communication with the new mine. They found themselves at the beginning of a tolerably wide gallery. One might well believe that it had been pierced by the hand of man, that the pick and mattock had emptied it in the working of a new vein. The explorers question whether, by a strange chance, they had not been transported into some ancient mine, of the existence of which even the oldest miners in the county had ever known.

No! It was merely that the geological layers had left this passage when the secondary earths were in course of formation. Perhaps some torrent had formerly dashed through it; but now it was as dry as if it had been cut some thousand feet lower, through granite rocks. At the same time, the air circulated freely, which showed that certain natural vents placed it in communication with the exterior atmosphere.

This observation, made by the engineer, was correct, and it was evident that the ventilation of the new mine would be easily managed. As to the fire-damp which had lately filtered through the schist, it seemed to have been contained in a pocket now empty, and it was certain that the atmosphere of the gallery was quite free from it. However, Harry prudently carried only the safety lamp, which would insure light for twelve hours.

James Starr and his companions now felt perfectly happy. All their wishes were satisfied. There was nothing but coal around them. A sort of emotion kept them silent; even Simon Ford restrained himself. His joy overflowed, not in long phrases, but in short ejaculations.

It was perhaps imprudent to venture so far into the crypt. Pooh! they never thought of how they were to get back.

The gallery was practicable, not very winding. They met with no noxious exhalations, nor did any chasm bar the path. There was no reason for stopping for a whole hour; James Starr, Madge, Harry, and Simon Ford walked on, though there was nothing to show them what was the exact direction of this unknown tunnel.

And they would no doubt have gone farther still, if they had not suddenly come to the end of the wide road which they had followed since their entrance into the mine.

The gallery ended in an enormous cavern, neither the height nor depth of which could be calculated. At what altitude arched the roof of this excavation—at what distance was its opposite wall—the darkness totally concealed; but by the light of the lamp the explorers could discover that its dome covered a vast extent of still water—pond or lake—whose picturesque rocky banks were lost in obscurity.

"Halt!" exclaimed Ford, stopping suddenly. "Another step, and perhaps we shall fall into some fathomless pit."

"Let us rest awhile, then, my friends," returned the engineer. "Besides, we ought to be thinking of returning to the cottage."

"Our lamp will give light for another ten hours, sir," said Harry.

"Well, let us make a halt," replied Starr; "I confess my legs have need of a rest. And you, Madge, don't you feel tired after so long a walk?"

"Not over much, Mr. Starr," replied the sturdy Scotchwoman; "we have been accustomed to explore the old Aberfoyle mine for whole days together."

"Tired? nonsense!" interrupted Simon Ford; "Madge could go ten times as far, if necessary. But once more, Mr. Starr, wasn't my communication worth your trouble in coming to hear it? Just dare to say no, Mr. Starr, dare to say no!"

"Well, my old friend, I haven't felt so happy for a long while!" replied the engineer; "the small part of this marvelous mine that we have explored seems to show that its extent is very considerable, at least in length."

"In width and in depth, too, Mr. Starr!" returned Simon Ford.

"That we shall know later."

"And I can answer for it! Trust to the instinct of an old miner! It has never deceived me!"

"I wish to believe you, Simon," replied the engineer, smiling. "As far as I can judge from this short exploration, we possess the elements of a working which will last for centuries!"

"Centuries!" exclaimed Simon Ford; "I believe you, sir! A thousand years and more will pass before the last bit of coal is taken out of our new mine!"

"Heaven grant it!" returned Starr. "As to the quality of the coal which crops out of these walls?"

"Superb! Mr. Starr, superb!" answered Ford; "just look at it yourself!"

And so saying, with his pick he struck off a fragment of the black rock.

"Look! look!" he repeated, holding it close to his lamp; "the surface of this piece of coal is shining! We have here fat coal, rich in bituminous matter; and see how it comes in pieces, almost without dust! Ah, Mr. Starr! twenty years ago this seam would have entered into a strong competition with Swansea and Cardiff! Well, stokers will quarrel for it still, and if it costs little to extract it from the mine, it will not sell at a less price outside."

"Indeed," said Madge, who had taken the fragment of coal and was examining it with the air of a connoisseur; "that's good quality of coal. Carry it home, Simon, carry it back to the cottage! I want this first piece of coal to burn under our kettle."

"Well said, wife!" answered the old overman, "and you shall see that I am not mistaken."

"Mr. Starr," asked Harry, "have you any idea of the probable direction of this long passage which we have been following since our entrance into the new mine?"

"No, my lad," replied the engineer; "with a compass I could perhaps find out its general bearing; but without a compass I am here like a sailor in open sea, in the midst of fogs, when there is no sun by which to calculate his position."

"No doubt, Mr. Starr," replied Ford; "but pray don't compare our position with that of the sailor, who has everywhere and always an abyss under his feet! We are on firm ground here, and need never be afraid of foundering."

"I won't tease you, then, old Simon," answered James Starr. "Far be it from me even in jest to depreciate the New Aberfoyle mine by an unjust comparison! I only meant to say one thing, and that is that we don't know where we are."

"We are in the subsoil of the county of Stirling, Mr. Starr," replied Simon Ford; "and that I assert as if—"

"Listen!" said Harry, interrupting the old man. All listened, as the young miner was doing. His ears, which were very sharp, had caught a dull sound, like a distant murmur. His companions were not long in hearing it themselves. It was above their heads, a sort of rolling sound, in which though it was so feeble, the successive *crescendo* and *diminuendo* could be distinctly heard.

All four stood for some minutes, their ears on the stretch, without uttering a word. All at once Simon Ford exclaimed, "Well, I declare! Are trucks already running on the rails of New Aberfoyle?"

"Father," replied Harry, "it sounds to me just like the noise made by waves rolling on the sea shore."

"We can't be under the sea though!" cried the old overman.

"No," said the engineer, "but it is not impossible that we should be under Loch Katrine."

"The roof cannot have much thickness just here, if the noise of the water is perceptible."

"Very little indeed," answered James Starr, "and that is the reason this cavern is so huge."

"You must be right, Mr. Starr," said Harry.

"Besides, the weather is so bad outside," resumed Starr, "that the waters of the loch must be as rough as those of the Firth of Forth."

"Well! what does it matter after all?" returned Simon Ford; "the seam won't be any the worse because it is under a loch. It would not be the first time that coal has been looked for under the very bed of the ocean! When we have to work under the bottom of the Caledonian Canal, where will be the harm?"

"Well said, Simon," cried the engineer, who could not restrain a smile at the overman's enthusiasm; "let us cut our trenches under the waters of the sea! Let us bore the bed of the Atlantic like a strainer; let us with our picks join our brethren of the United States through the subsoil of the ocean! let us dig into the center of the globe if necessary, to tear out the last scrap of coal."

"Are you joking, Mr. Starr?" asked Ford, with a pleased but slightly suspicious look.

"I joking, old man? no! but you are so enthusiastic that you carry me away into the regions of impossibility! Come, let us return to the reality, which is sufficiently beautiful; leave our picks here, where we may find them another day, and let's take the road back to the cottage."

Nothing more could be done for the time. Later, the engineer, accompanied by a brigade of miners, supplied with lamps and all necessary tools, would resume the exploration of New Aberfoyle. It was now time to return to the Dochart pit. The road was easy, the gallery running nearly straight through the rock up to the orifice opened by the dynamite, so there was no fear of their losing themselves.

But as James Starr was proceeding towards the gallery Simon Ford stopped him.

"Mr. Starr," said he, "you see this immense cavern, this subterranean lake, whose waters bathe this strand at our feet? Well! it is to this place I mean to change my dwelling, here I will build a new cottage, and if some brave fellows will follow my example, before a year is over there will be one town more inside old England."

James Starr, smiling approval of Ford's plans, pressed his hand, and all three, preceding Madge, re-entered the gallery, on their way back to the Dochart pit. For the first mile no incident occurred. Harry walked first, holding his lamp above his head. He carefully followed the principal gallery, without ever turning aside into the narrow tunnels which radiated to the right and left. It seemed as if the returning was to be accomplished as easily as the going, when an unexpected accident occurred which rendered the situation of the explorers very serious.

Just at a moment when Harry was raising his lamp there came a rush of air, as if caused by the flapping of invisible wings. The lamp escaped from his hands, fell on the rocky ground, and was broken to pieces.

James Starr and his companions were suddenly plunged in absolute darkness. All the oil of the lamp was spilt, and it was of no further use. "Well, Harry," cried his father, "do you want us all to break our necks on the way back to the cottage?"

Harry did not answer. He wondered if he ought to suspect the hand of a mysterious being in this last accident? Could there possibly exist in these depths an enemy whose unaccountable antagonism would one day create serious difficulties? Had someone an interest in defending the new coal field against any attempt at working it? In truth that seemed absurd, yet the facts spoke for themselves, and they accumulated in such a way as to change simple presumptions into certainties.

In the meantime the explorers' situation was bad enough. They had now, in the midst of black darkness, to follow the passage leading to the Dochart pit for nearly five miles. There they would still have an hour's walk before reaching the cottage.

"Come along," said Simon Ford. "We have no time to lose. We must grope our way along, like blind men. There's no fear of losing our way. The tunnels which open off our road are only just like those in a molehill, and by following the chief gallery we shall of course reach the opening we got in at. After that, it is the old mine. We know that, and it won't be the first time that Harry and I have found ourselves there in the dark. Besides, there we shall find the lamps that we left. Forward then! Harry, go first. Mr. Starr, follow him. Madge, you go next, and I will bring up the rear. Above everything, don't let us get separated."

All complied with the old overman's instructions. As he said, by groping carefully, they could not mistake the way. It was only necessary to make the hands take the place of the eyes, and to trust to their instinct, which had with Simon Ford and his son become a second nature.

James Starr and his companions walked on in the order agreed. They did not speak, but it was not for want of thinking. It became evident that they had an adversary. But what was he, and how were they to defend themselves against these mysteriously-prepared attacks? These disquieting ideas crowded into their brains. However, this was not the moment to get discouraged.

Harry, his arms extended, advanced with a firm step, touching first one and then the other side of the passage.

If a cleft or side opening presented itself, he felt with his hand that it was not the main way; either the cleft was too shallow, or the opening too narrow, and he thus kept in the right road.

In darkness through which the eye could not in the slightest degree pierce, this difficult return lasted two hours. By reckoning the time since they started, taking into consideration that the walking had not been rapid, Starr calculated that he and his companions were near the opening. In fact, almost immediately, Harry stopped.

"Have we got to the end of the gallery?" asked Simon Ford.

"Yes," answered the young miner.

"Well! have you not found the hole which connects New Aberfoyle with the Dochart pit?"

"No," replied Harry, whose impatient hands met with nothing but a solid wall.

The old overman stepped forward, and himself felt the schistous rock. A cry escaped him.

Either the explorers had strayed from the right path on their return, or the narrow orifice, broken in the rock by the dynamite, had been recently stopped up. James Starr and his companions were prisoners in New Aberfoyle.

***

## CHAPTER IX

## THE FIRE-MAIDENS

A week after the events just related had taken place, James Starr's friends had become very anxious. The engineer had disappeared, and no reason could be brought forward to explain his absence. They learnt, by questioning his servant, that he had embarked at Granton Pier. But from that time there were no traces of James Starr. Simon Ford's letter had requested secrecy, and he had said nothing of his departure for the Aberfoyle mines.

Therefore in Edinburgh nothing was talked of but the unaccountable absence of the engineer. Sir W. Elphiston, the President of the Royal Institution, communicated to his colleagues a letter which James Starr had sent him, excusing himself from being present at the next meeting of the society. Two or three others produced similar letters. But though these documents proved that Starr had left Edinburgh—which was known before—they threw no light on what had become of him. Now, on the part of such a man, this prolonged absence, so contrary to his usual habits, naturally first caused surprise, and then anxiety.

A notice was inserted in the principal newspapers of the United Kingdom relative to the engineer James Starr, giving a description of him and the date on which he left Edinburgh; nothing more could be done but to wait. The time passed in great anxiety. The scientific world of England was inclined to believe that one of its most distinguished members had positively disappeared. At the same time, when so many people were thinking about James Starr, Harry Ford was the subject of no less anxiety. Only, instead of occupying public attention, the son of the old overman was the cause of trouble alone to the generally cheerful mind of Jack Ryan.

It may be remembered that, in their encounter in the Yarrow shaft, Jack Ryan had invited Harry to come a week afterwards to the festivities at Irvine. Harry had accepted and promised expressly to be there. Jack Ryan knew, having had it proved by many circumstances, that his friend was a man of his word. With him, a thing promised was a thing done. Now, at the Irvine merry-making, nothing was wanting; neither song, nor dance, nor fun of any sort—nothing but Harry Ford.

The notice relative to James Starr, published in the papers, had not yet been seen by Ryan. The honest fellow was therefore only worried by Harry's absence, telling himself that something serious could alone have prevented him from keeping his promise. So, the day after the Irvine games, Jack Ryan intended to take the railway from Glasgow and go to the Dochart pit; and this he would have done had he not been detained by an accident which nearly cost him his life. Something which occurred on the night of the 12th of December was of a nature to support the opinions of all partisans of the supernatural, and there were many at Melrose Farm.

Irvine, a little seaport of Renfrew, containing nearly seven thousand inhabitants, lies in a sharp bend made by the Scottish coast, near the mouth of the Firth of Clyde. The most ancient and the most famed ruins on this part of the coast were those of this castle of Robert Stuart, which bore the name of Dundonald Castle.

At this period Dundonald Castle, a refuge for all the stray goblins of the country, was completely deserted. It stood on the top of a high rock, two miles from the town, and was seldom visited. Sometimes a few strangers took it into their heads to explore these old historical remains, but then they always went alone. The inhabitants of Irvine would not have taken them there at any price. Indeed, several legends were based on the story of certain "fire-maidens," who haunted the old castle.

The most superstitious declared they had seen these fantastic creatures with their own eyes. Jack Ryan was naturally one of them. It was a fact that from time to time long flames appeared, sometimes on a broken piece of wall, sometimes on the summit of the tower which was the highest point of Dundonald Castle.

Did these flames really assume a human shape, as was asserted? Did they merit the name of fire-maidens, given them by the people of the coast? It was evidently just an optical delusion, aided by a good deal of credulity, and science could easily have explained the phenomenon.

However that might be, these fire-maidens had the reputation of frequenting the ruins of the old castle and there performing wild strathspeys, especially on dark nights. Jack Ryan, bold fellow though he was, would never have dared to accompany those dances with the music of his bagpipes.

"Old Nick is enough for them!" said he. "He doesn't need me to complete his infernal orchestra."

We may well believe that these strange apparitions frequently furnished a text for the evening stories. Jack Ryan was ending the evening with one of these. His auditors, transported into the phantom world, were worked up into a state of mind which would believe anything.

All at once shouts were heard outside. Jack Ryan stopped short in the middle of his story, and all rushed out of the barn. The night was pitchy dark. Squalls of wind and rain swept along the beach. Two or three fishermen, their backs against a rock, the better to resist the wind, were shouting at the top of their voices.

Jack Ryan and his companions ran up to them. The shouts were, however, not for the inhabitants of the farm, but to warn men who, without being aware of it, were going to destruction. A dark, confused mass appeared some way out at sea. It was a vessel whose position could be seen by her lights, for she carried a white one on her foremast, a green on the starboard side, and a red on the outside. She was evidently running straight on the rocks.

"A ship in distress?" said Ryan.

"Ay," answered one of the fishermen, "and now they want to tack, but it's too late!"

"Do they want to run ashore?" said another.

"It seems so," responded one of the fishermen, "unless he has been misled by some—"

The man was interrupted by a yell from Jack. Could the crew have heard it? At any rate, it was too late for them to beat back from the line of breakers which gleamed white in the darkness.

But it was not, as might be supposed, a last effort of Ryan's to warn the doomed ship. He now had his back to the sea. His companions turned also, and gazed at a spot situated about half a mile inland. It was Dundonald Castle. A long flame twisted and bent under the gale, on the summit of the old tower.

"The Fire-Maiden!" cried the superstitious men in terror.

Clearly, it needed a good strong imagination to find any human likeness in that flame. Waving in the wind like a luminous flag, it seemed sometimes to fly round the tower, as if it was just going out, and a moment after it was seen again dancing on its blue point.

"The Fire-Maiden! the Fire-Maiden!" cried the terrified fishermen and peasants.

All was then explained. The ship, having lost her reckoning in the fog, had taken this flame on the top of Dundonald Castle for the Irvine light. She thought herself at the entrance of the Firth, ten miles to the north, when she was really running on a shore which offered no refuge.

What could be done to save her, if there was still time? It was too late. A frightful crash was heard above the tumult of the elements. The vessel had struck. The white line of surf was broken for an instant; she heeled over on her side and lay among the rocks.

At the same time, by a strange coincidence, the long flame disappeared, as if it had been swept away by a violent gust. Earth, sea, and sky were plunged in complete darkness.

"The Fire-Maiden!" shouted Ryan, for the last time, as the apparition, which he and his companions believed supernatural, disappeared. But then the courage of these superstitious Scotchmen, which had failed before a fancied danger, returned in face of a real one, which they were ready to brave in order to save their fellow-creatures. The tempest did not deter them. As heroic as they had before been credulous, fastening ropes round their waists, they rushed into the waves to the aid of those on the wreck.

Happily, they succeeded in their endeavors, although some—and bold Jack Ryan was among the number—were severely wounded on the rocks. But the captain of the vessel and the eight sailors who composed his crew were hauled up, safe and sound, on the beach.

The ship was the Norwegian brig *Motala*, laden with timber, and bound for Glasgow. Of the *Motala* herself nothing remained but a few spars, washed up by the waves, and dashed among the rocks on the beach.

Jack Ryan and three of his companions, wounded like himself, were carried into a room of Melrose Farm, where every care was lavished on them. Ryan was the most hurt, for when with the rope round his waist he had rushed into the sea, the waves had almost immediately dashed him back against the rocks. He was brought, indeed, very nearly lifeless on to the beach.

The brave fellow was therefore confined to bed for several days, to his great disgust. However, as soon as he was given permission to sing as much as he liked, he bore his trouble patiently, and the farm echoed all day with his jovial voice. But from this adventure he imbibed a more lively sentiment of fear with regard to brownies and other goblins who amuse themselves by plaguing mankind, and he made them responsible for the catastrophe of the Motala. It would have been vain to try and convince him that the Fire-Maidens did not exist, and that the flame, so suddenly appearing among the ruins, was but a natural phenomenon. No reasoning could make him believe it. His companions were, if possible, more obstinate than he in their credulity. According to them, one of the Fire-Maidens had maliciously attracted the *Motala* to the coast. As to wishing to punish her, as well try to bring the tempest to justice! The magistrates might order what arrests they pleased, but a flame cannot be imprisoned, an impalpable being can't be handcuffed. It must be acknowledged that the researches which were ultimately made gave ground, at least in appearance, to this superstitious way of explaining the facts.

The inquiry was made with great care. Officials came to Dundonald Castle, and they proceeded to conduct a most vigorous search. The magistrate wished first to ascertain if the ground bore any footprints, which could be attributed to other than goblins' feet. It was impossible to find the least trace, whether old or new. Moreover, the earth, still damp from the rain of the day before, would have preserved the least vestige.

The result of all this was, that the magistrates only got for their trouble a new legend added to so many others—a legend which would be perpetuated by the remembrance of the catastrophe of the *Motala*, and indisputably confirm the truth of the apparition of the Fire-Maidens.

A hearty fellow like Jack Ryan, with so strong a constitution, could not be long confined to his bed. A few sprains and bruises were not quite enough to keep him on his back longer than he liked. He had not time to be ill.

Jack, therefore, soon got well. As soon as he was on his legs again, before resuming his work on the farm, he wished to go and visit his friend Harry, and learn why he had not come to the Irvine merry-making. He could not understand his absence, for Harry was not a man who would willingly promise and not perform. It was unlikely, too, that the son of the old overman had not heard of the wreck of the *Motala*, as it was in all the papers. He must know the part Jack had taken in it, and what had happened to him, and it was unlike Harry not to hasten to the farm and see how his old chum was going on.

As Harry had not come, there must have been something to prevent him. Jack Ryan would as soon deny the existence of the Fire-Maidens as believe in Harry's indifference.

Two days after the catastrophe Jack left the farm merily, feeling nothing of his wounds. Singing in the fullness of his heart, he awoke the echoes of the cliff, as he walked to the station of the railway, which *via* Glasgow would take him to Stirling and Callander.

As he was waiting for his train, his attention was attracted by a bill posted up on the walls, containing the following notice:

"On the 4th of December, the engineer, James Starr, of Edinburgh, embarked from Granton Pier, on board the *Prince of Wales*. He disembarked the same day at Stirling. From that time nothing further has been heard of him.

"Any information concerning him is requested to be sent to the President of the Royal Institution, Edinburgh."

Jack Ryan, stopping before one of these advertisements, read it twice over, with extreme surprise.

"Mr. Starr!" he exclaimed. "Why, on the 4th of December I met him with Harry on the ladder of the Dochart pit! That was ten days ago! And he has not been seen from that time! That explains why my chum didn't come to Irvine."

And without taking time to inform the President of the Royal Institution by letter, what he knew relative to James Starr, Jack jumped into the train, determining to go first of all to the Yarrow shaft. There he would descend to the depths of the pit, if necessary, to find Harry, and with him was sure to be the engineer James Starr.

"They haven't turned up again," said he to himself. "Why? Has anything prevented them? Could any work of importance keep them still at the bottom of the mine? I must find out!" and Ryan, hastening his steps, arrived in less than an hour at the Yarrow shaft.

Externally nothing was changed. The same silence around. Not a living creature was moving in that desert region. Jack entered the ruined shed which covered the opening of the shaft. He gazed down into the dark abyss—nothing was to be seen. He listened—nothing was to be heard.

"And my lamp!" he exclaimed; "suppose it isn't in its place!" The lamp which Ryan used when he visited the pit was usually deposited in a corner, near the landing of the topmost ladder. It had disappeared.

"Here is a nuisance!" said Jack, beginning to feel rather uneasy. Then, without hesitating, superstitious though he was, "I will go," said he, "though it's as dark down there as in the lowest depths of the infernal regions!"

And he began to descend the long flight of ladders, which led down the gloomy shaft. Jack Ryan had not forgotten his old mining habits, and he was well acquainted with the Dochart pit, or he would scarcely have dared to venture thus. He went very carefully, however. His foot tried each round, as some of them were worm-eaten. A false step would entail a deadly fall, through this space of fifteen hundred feet. He counted each landing as he passed it, knowing that he could not reach the bottom of the shaft until he had left the thirtieth. Once there, he would have no trouble, so he thought, in finding the cottage, built, as we have said, at the extremity of the principal passage.

Jack Ryan went on thus until he got to the twenty-sixth landing, and consequently had two hundred feet between him and the bottom.

Here he put down his leg to feel for the first rung of the twenty-seventh ladder. But his foot swinging in space found nothing to rest on. He knelt down and felt about with his hand for the top of the ladder. It was in vain.

"Old Nick himself must have been down this way!" said Jack, not without a slight feeling of terror.

He stood considering for some time, with folded arms, and longing to be able to pierce the impenetrable darkness. Then it occurred to him that if he could not get down, neither could the inhabitants of the mine get up. There was now no communication between the depths of the pit and the upper regions. If the removal of the lower ladders of the Yarrow shaft had been effected since his last visit to the cottage, what had become of Simon Ford, his wife, his son, and the engineer?

The prolonged absence of James Starr proved that he had not left the pit since the day Ryan met with him in the shaft. How had the cottage been provisioned since then? The food of these unfortunate people, imprisoned fifteen hundred feet below the surface of the ground, must have been exhausted by this time.

All this passed through Jack's mind, as he saw that by himself he could do nothing to get to the cottage. He had no doubt but that communication had been interrupted with a malevolent intention. At any rate, the authorities must be informed, and that as soon as possible. Jack Ryan bent forward from the landing.

"Harry! Harry!" he shouted with his powerful voice.

Harry's name echoed and re-echoed among the rocks, and finally died away in the depths of the shaft.

Ryan rapidly ascended the upper ladders and returned to the light of day. Without losing a moment he reached the Callander station, just caught the express to Edinburgh, and by three o'clock was before the Lord Provost.

There his declaration was received. His account was given so clearly that it could not be doubted. Sir William Elphiston, President of the Royal Institution, and not only colleague, but a personal friend of Starr's, was also informed, and asked to direct the search which was to be made without delay in the mine. Several men were placed at his disposal, supplied with lamps, picks, long rope ladders, not forgetting provisions and cordials. Then guided by Jack Ryan, the party set out for the Aberfoyle mines.

The same evening the expedition arrived at the opening of the Yarrow shaft, and descended to the twenty-seventh landing, at which Jack Ryan had been stopped a few hours previously. The lamps, fastened to long ropes, were lowered down the shaft, and it was thus ascertained that the four last ladders were wanting.

As soon as the lamps had been brought up, the men fixed to the landing a rope ladder, which unrolled itself down the shaft, and all descended one after the other. Jack Ryan's descent was the most difficult, for he went first down the swinging ladders, and fastened them for the others.

The space at the bottom of the shaft was completely deserted; but Sir William was much surprised at hearing Jack Ryan exclaim, "Here are bits of the ladders, and some of them half burnt!"

"Burnt?" repeated Sir William. "Indeed, here sure enough are cinders which have evidently been cold a long time!"

"Do you think, sir," asked Ryan, "that Mr. Starr could have had any reason for burning the ladders, and thus breaking of communication with the world?"

"Certainly not," answered Sir William Elphiston, who had become very thoughtful. "Come, my lad, lead us to the cottage. There we shall ascertain the truth."

Jack Ryan shook his head, as if not at all convinced. Then, taking a lamp from the hands of one of the men, he proceeded with a rapid step along the principal passage of the Dochart pit. The others all followed him.

In a quarter of an hour the party arrived at the excavation in which stood Simon Ford's cottage. There was no light in the window. Ryan darted to the door, and threw it open. The house was empty.

They examined all the rooms in the somber habitation. No trace of violence was to be found. All was in order, as if old Madge had been still there. There was even an ample supply of provisions, enough to last the Ford family for several days.

The absence of the tenants of the cottage was quite unaccountable. But was it not possible to find out the exact time they had quitted it? Yes, for in this region, where there was no difference of day or night, Madge was accustomed to mark with a cross each day in her almanac.

The almanac was pinned up on the wall, and there the last cross had been made at the 6th of December; that is to say, a day after the arrival of James Starr, to which Ryan could positively swear. It was clear that on the 6th of December, ten days ago, Simon Ford, his wife, son, and guest, had quitted the cottage. Could a fresh exploration of the mine, undertaken by the engineer, account for such a long absence? Certainly not.

It was intensely dark all round. The lamps held by the men gave light only just where they were standing. Suddenly Jack Ryan uttered a cry. "Look there, there!"

His finger was pointing to a tolerably bright light, which was moving about in the distance. "After that light, my men!" exclaimed Sir William.

"It's a goblin light!" said Ryan. "So what's the use? We shall never catch it."

The president and his men, little given to superstition, darted off in the direction of the moving light. Jack Ryan, bravely following their example, quickly overtook the head-most of the party.

It was a long and fatiguing chase. The lantern seemed to be carried by a being of small size, but singular agility.

Every now and then it disappeared behind some pillar, then was seen again at the end of a cross gallery. A sharp turn would place it out of sight, and it seemed to have completely disappeared, when all at once there would be the light as bright as ever. However, they gained very little on it, and Ryan's belief that they could never catch it seemed far from groundless.

After an hour of this vain pursuit Sir William Elphiston and his companions had gone a long way in the southwest direction of the pit, and began to think they really had to do with an impalpable being. Just then it seemed as if the distance between the goblin and those who were pursuing it was becoming less. Could it be fatigued, or did this invisible being wish to entice Sir William and his companions to the place where the inhabitants of the cottage had perhaps themselves been enticed. It was hard to say.

The men, seeing that the distance lessened, redoubled their efforts. The light which had before burnt at a distance of more than two hundred feet before them was now seen at less than fifty. The space continued to diminish. The bearer of the lamp became partially visible. Sometimes, when it turned its head, the indistinct profile of a human face could be made out, and unless a sprite could assume bodily shape, Jack Ryan was obliged to confess that here was no supernatural being. Then, springing forward,—

"Courage, comrades!" he exclaimed; "it is getting tired! We shall soon catch it up now, and if it can talk as well as it can run we shall hear a fine story."

But the pursuit had suddenly become more difficult. They were in unknown regions of the mine; narrow passages crossed each other like the windings of a labyrinth. The bearer of the lamp might escape them as easily as possible, by just extinguishing the light and retreating into some dark refuge.

"And indeed," thought Sir William, "if it wishes to avoid us, why does it not do so?"

Hitherto there had evidently been no intention to avoid them, but just as the thought crossed Sir William's mind the light suddenly disappeared, and the party, continuing the pursuit, found themselves before an extremely narrow natural opening in the schistous rocks.

To trim their lamps, spring forward, and dart through the opening, was for Sir William and his party but the work of an instant. But before they had gone a hundred paces along this new gallery, much wider and loftier than the former, they all stopped short. There, near the wall, lay four bodies, stretched on the ground—four corpses, perhaps!

"James Starr!" exclaimed Sir William Elphiston.

"Harry! Harry!" cried Ryan, throwing himself down beside his friend.

It was indeed the engineer, Madge, Simon, and Harry Ford who were lying there motionless. But one of the bodies moved slightly, and Madge's voice was heard faintly murmuring, "See to the others! help them first!"

Sir William, Jack, and their companions endeavored to reanimate the engineer and his friends by getting them to swallow a few drops of brandy. They very soon succeeded. The unfortunate people, shut up in that dark cavern for ten days, were dying of starvation. They must have perished had they not on three occasions found a loaf of bread and a jug of water set near them. No doubt the charitable being to whom they owed their lives was unable to do more for them.

Sir William wondered whether this might not have been the work of the strange sprite who had allured them to the very spot where James Starr and his companions lay.

However that might be, the engineer, Madge, Simon, and Harry Ford were saved. They were assisted to the cottage, passing through the narrow opening which the bearer of the strange light had apparently wished to point out to Sir William. This was a natural opening. The passage which James Starr and his companions had made for themselves with dynamite had been completely blocked up with rocks laid one upon another.

So, then, whilst they had been exploring the vast cavern, the way back had been purposely closed against them by a hostile hand.

***

## CHAPTER X

## COAL TOWN

Three years after the events which have just been related, the guide-books recommended as a "great attraction," to the numerous tourists who roam over the county of Stirling, a visit of a few hours to the mines of New Aberfoyle.

No mine in any country, either in the Old or New World, could present a more curious aspect.

To begin with, the visitor was transported without danger or fatigue to a level with the workings, at fifteen hundred feet below the surface of the ground. Seven miles to the southwest of Callander opened a slanting tunnel, adorned with a castellated entrance, turrets and battlements. This lofty tunnel gently sloped straight to the stupendous crypt, hollowed out so strangely in the bowels of the earth.

A double line of railway, the wagons being moved by hydraulic power, plied from hour to hour to and from the village thus buried in the subsoil of the county, and which bore the rather ambitious title of Coal Town.

Arrived in Coal Town, the visitor found himself in a place where electricity played a principal part as an agent of heat and light. Although the ventilation shafts were numerous, they were not sufficient to admit much daylight into New Aberfoyle, yet it had abundance of light. This was shed from numbers of electric discs; some suspended from the vaulted roofs, others hanging on the natural pillars—all, whether suns or stars in size, were fed by continuous currents produced from electro-magnetic machines. When the hour of rest arrived, an artificial night was easily produced all over the mine by disconnecting the wires.

Below the dome lay a lake of an extent to be compared to the Dead Sea of the Mammoth caves—a deep lake whose transparent waters swarmed with eyeless fish, and to which the engineer gave the name of Loch Malcolm.

There, in this immense natural excavation, Simon Ford built his new cottage, which he would not have exchanged for the finest house in Prince's Street, Edinburgh. This dwelling was situated on the shores of the loch, and its five windows looked out on the dark waters, which extended further than the eye could see. Two months later a second habitation was erected in the neighborhood of Simon Ford's cottage: this was for James Starr. The engineer had given himself body and soul to New Aberfoyle, and nothing but the most imperative necessity ever caused him to leave the pit. There, then, he lived in the midst of his mining world.

On the discovery of the new field, all the old colliers had hastened to leave the plow and harrow, and resume the pick and mattock. Attracted by the certainty that work would never fail, allured by the high wages which the prosperity of the mine enabled the company to offer for labor, they deserted the open air for an underground life, and took up their abode in the mines.

The miners' houses, built of brick, soon grew up in a picturesque fashion; some on the banks of Loch Malcolm, others under the arches which seemed made to resist the weight that pressed upon them, like the piers of a bridge. So was founded Coal Town, situated under the eastern point of Loch Katrine, to the north of the county of Stirling. It was a regular settlement on the banks of Loch Malcolm. A chapel, dedicated to St. Giles, overlooked it from the top of a huge rock, whose foot was laved by the waters of the subterranean sea.

When this underground town was lighted up by the bright rays thrown from the discs, hung from the pillars and arches, its aspect was so strange, so fantastic, that it justified the praise of the guide-books, and visitors flocked to see it.

It is needless to say that the inhabitants of Coal Town were proud of their place. They rarely left their laboring village—in that imitating

Simon Ford, who never wished to go out again. The old overman maintained that it always rained "up there," and, considering the climate of the United Kingdom, it must be acknowledged that he was not far wrong. All the families in New Aberfoyle prospered well, having in three years obtained a certain competency which they could never have hoped to attain on the surface of the county. Dozens of babies, who were born at the time when the works were resumed, had never yet breathed the outer air.

This made Jack Ryan remark, "It's eighteen months since they were weaned, and they have not yet seen daylight!"

It may be mentioned here, that one of the first to run at the engineer's call was Jack Ryan. The merry fellow had thought it his duty to return to his old trade. But though Melrose farm had lost singer and piper it must not be thought that Jack Ryan sung no more. On the contrary, the sonorous echoes of New Aberfoyle exerted their strong lungs to answer him.

Jack Ryan took up his abode in Simon Ford's new cottage. They offered him a room, which he accepted without ceremony, in his frank and hearty way. Old Madge loved him for his fine character and good nature. She in some degree shared his ideas on the subject of the fantastic beings who were supposed to haunt the mine, and the two, when alone, told each other stories wild enough to make one shudder—stories well worthy of enriching the hyperborean mythology.

Jack thus became the life of the cottage. He was, besides being a jovial companion, a good workman. Six months after the works had begun, he was made head of a gang of hewers.

"That was a good work done, Mr. Ford," said he, a few days after his appointment. "You discovered a new field, and though you narrowly escaped paying for the discovery with your life—well, it was not too dearly bought."

"No, Jack, it was a good bargain we made that time!" answered the old overman. "But neither Mr. Starr nor I have forgotten that to you we owe our lives."

"Not at all," returned Jack. "You owe them to your son Harry, when he had the good sense to accept my invitation to Irvine."

"And not to go, isn't that it?" interrupted Harry, grasping his comrade's hand. "No, Jack, it is to you, scarcely healed of your wounds—to you, who did not delay a day, no, nor an hour, that we owe our being found still alive in the mine!"

"Rubbish, no!" broke in the obstinate fellow. "I won't have that said, when it's no such thing. I hurried to find out what had become of you, Harry, that's all. But to give everyone his due, I will add that without that unapproachable goblin—"

"Ah, there we are!" cried Ford. "A goblin!"

"A goblin, a brownie, a fairy's child," repeated Jack Ryan, "a cousin of the Fire-Maidens, an Urisk, whatever you like! It's not the less certain that without it we should never have found our way into the gallery, from which you could not get out."

"No doubt, Jack," answered Harry. "It remains to be seen whether this being was as supernatural as you choose to believe."

"Supernatural!" exclaimed Ryan. "But it was as supernatural as a Will-o'-the-Wisp, who may be seen skipping along with his lantern in his hand; you may try to catch him, but he escapes like a fairy, and vanishes like a shadow! Don't be uneasy, Harry, we shall see it again some day or other!"

"Well, Jack," said Simon Ford, "Will-o'-the-Wisp or not, we shall try to find it, and you must help us."

"You'll get into a scrap if you don't take care, Mr. Ford!" responded Jack Ryan.

"We'll see about that, Jack!"

We may easily imagine how soon this domain of New Aberfoyle became familiar to all the members of the Ford family, but more particularly to Harry. He learnt to know all its most secret ins and outs. He could even say what point of the surface corresponded with what point of the mine. He knew that above this seam lay the Firth of Clyde, that there extended Loch Lomond and Loch Katrine. Those columns supported a spur of the Grampian mountains. This vault served as a basement to Dumbarton. Above this large pond passed the Balloch railway. Here ended the Scottish coast. There began the sea, the tumult of which could be distinctly heard during the equinoctial gales. Harry would have been a first-rate guide to these natural catacombs, and all that Alpine guides do on their snowy peaks in daylight he could have done in the dark mine by the wonderful power of instinct.

He loved New Aberfoyle. Many times, with his lamp stuck in his hat, did he penetrate its furthest depths. He explored its ponds in a skillfully-managed canoe. He even went shooting, for numerous birds had been introduced into the crypt—pintails, snipes, ducks, who fed on the fish which swarmed in the deep waters. Harry's eyes seemed made for the dark, just as a sailor's are made for distances. But all this while Harry felt irresistibly animated by the hope of finding the mysterious being whose intervention, strictly speaking, had saved himself and his friends. Would he succeed? He certainly would, if presentiments were to be trusted; but certainly not, if he judged by the success which had as yet attended his researches.

The attacks directed against the family of the old overman, before the discovery of New Aberfoyle, had not been renewed.

***

# CHAPTER XI

## HANGING BY A THREAD

Although in this way the Ford family led a happy and contented life, yet it was easy to see that Harry, naturally of a grave disposition, became more and more quiet and reserved. Even Jack Ryan, with all his good humor and usually infectious merriment, failed to rouse him to gayety of manner.

One Sunday—it was in the month of June—the two friends were walking together on the shores of Loch Malcolm. Coal Town rested from labor. In the world above, stormy weather prevailed. Violent rains fell, and dull sultry vapors brooded over the earth; the atmosphere was most oppressive.

Down in Coal Town there was perfect calm; no wind, no rain. A soft and pleasant temperature existed instead of the strife of the elements which raged without. What wonder then, that excursionists from Stirling came in considerable numbers to enjoy the calm fresh air in the recesses of the mine?

The electric discs shed a brilliancy of light which the British sun, oftener obscured by fogs than it ought to be, might well envy. Jack Ryan kept talking of these visitors, who passed them in noisy crowds, but Harry paid very little attention to what he said.

"I say, do look, Harry!" cried Jack. "See what numbers of people come to visit us! Cheer up, old fellow! Do the honors of the place a little better. If you look so glum, you'll make all these outside folks think you envy their life above-ground."

"Never mind me, Jack," answered Harry. "You are jolly enough for two, I'm sure; that's enough."

"I'll be hanged if I don't feel your melancholy creeping over me though!" exclaimed Jack. "I declare my eyes are getting quite dull, my lips are drawn together, my laugh sticks in my throat; I'm forgetting all my songs. Come, man, what's the matter with you?"

"You know well enough, Jack."

"What? the old story?"

"Yes, the same thoughts haunt me."

"Ah, poor fellow!" said Jack, shrugging his shoulders. "If you would only do like me, and set all the queer things down to the account of the goblins of the mine, you would be easier in your mind."

"But, Jack, you know very well that these goblins exist only in your imagination, and that, since the works here have been reopened, not a single one has been seen."

"That's true, Harry; but if no spirits have been seen, neither has anyone else to whom you could attribute the extraordinary doings we want to account for."

"I shall discover them."

"Ah, Harry! Harry! it's not so easy to catch the spirits of New Aberfoyle!"

"I shall find out the spirits as you call them," said Harry, in a tone of firm conviction.

"Do you expect to be able to punish them?"

"Both punish and reward. Remember, if one hand shut us up in that passage, another hand delivered us! I shall not soon forget that."

"But, Harry, how can we be sure that these two hands do not belong to the same body?"

"What can put such a notion in your head, Jack?" asked Harry.

"Well, I don't know. Creatures that live in these holes, Harry, don't you see? they can't be made like us, eh?"

"But they *are* just like us, Jack."

"Oh, no! don't say that, Harry! Perhaps some madman managed to get in for a time."

"A madman! No madman would have formed such connected plans, or done such continued mischief as befell us after the breaking of the ladders."

"Well, but anyhow he has done no harm for the last three years, either to you, Harry, or any of your people."

"No matter, Jack," replied Harry; "I am persuaded that this malignant being, whoever he is, has by no means given up his evil intentions. I can hardly say on what I found my convictions. But at any rate, for the sake of the new works, I must and will know who he is and whence he comes."

"For the sake of the new works did you say?" asked Jack, considerably surprised.

"I said so, Jack," returned Harry. "I may be mistaken, but, to me, all that has happened proves the existence of an interest in this mine in strong opposition to ours. Many a time have I considered the matter; I feel almost sure of it. Just consider the whole series of inexplicable circumstances, so singularly linked together. To begin with, the anonymous letter, contradictory to that of my father, at once proves that some man had become aware of our projects, and wished to prevent their accomplishment. Mr. Starr comes to see us at the Dochart pit. No sooner does he enter it with me than an immense stone is cast upon us, and communication is interrupted by the breaking of the ladders in the Yarrow shaft. We commence exploring. An experiment, by which the existence of a new vein would be proved, is rendered impossible by stoppage of fissures. Notwithstanding this, the examination is carried out, the vein discovered. We return as we came, a prodigious gust of air meets us, our lamp is broken, utter darkness surrounds us. Nevertheless, we make our way along the gloomy passage until, on reaching the entrance, we find it blocked up. There we were—imprisoned. Now, Jack, don't you see in all these things a malicious intention? Ah, yes, believe me, some being hitherto invisible, but not supernatural, as you will persist in thinking, was concealed in the mine. For some reason, known only to himself, he strove to keep us out of it. *Was* there, did I say? I feel an inward conviction that he *is* there still, and probably prepares some terrible disaster for us. Even at the risk of my life, Jack, I am resolved to discover him."

Harry spoke with an earnestness which strongly impressed his companion. "Well, Harry," said he, "if I am forced to agree with you in certain points, won't you admit that some kind fairy or brownie, by bringing bread and water to you, was the means of—"

"Jack, my friend," interrupted Harry, "it is my belief that the friendly person, whom you will persist in calling a spirit, exists in the mine as certainly as the criminal we speak of, and I mean to seek them both in the most distant recesses of the mine."

"But," inquired Jack, "have you any possible clew to guide your search?"

"Perhaps I have. Listen to me! Five miles west of New Aberfoyle, under the solid rock which supports Ben Lomond, there exists a natural shaft which descends perpendicularly into the vein beneath. A week ago I went to ascertain the depth of this shaft. While sounding it, and bending over the opening as my plumb-line went down, it seemed to me that the air within was agitated, as though beaten by huge wings."

"Some bird must have got lost among the lower galleries," replied Jack.

"But that is not all, Jack. This very morning I went back to the place, and, listening attentively, I thought I could detect a sound like a sort of groaning."

"Groaning!" cried Jack, "that must be nonsense; it was a current of air—unless indeed some ghost—"

"I shall know to-morrow what it was," said Harry.

"To-morrow?" answered Jack, looking at his friend.

"Yes; to-morrow I am going down into that abyss."

"Harry! that will be a tempting of Providence."

"No, Jack, Providence will aid me in the attempt. Tomorrow, you and some of our comrades will go with me to that shaft. I will fasten myself to a long rope, by which you can let me down, and draw me up at a given signal. I may depend upon you, Jack?"

"Well, Harry," said Jack, shaking his head, "I will do as you wish me; but I tell you all the same, you are very wrong."

"Nothing venture nothing win," said Harry, in a tone of decision. "To-morrow morning, then, at six o'clock. Be silent, and farewell!"

It must be admitted that Jack Ryan's fears were far from groundless. Harry would expose himself to very great danger, supposing the enemy he sought for lay concealed at the bottom of the pit into which he was going to descend. It did not seem likely that such was the case, however.

"Why in the world," repeated Jack Ryan, "should he take all this trouble to account for a set of facts so very easily and simply explained by the supernatural intervention of the spirits of the mine?"

But, notwithstanding his objections to the scheme, Jack Ryan and three miners of his gang arrived next morning with Harry at the mouth of the opening of the suspicious shaft. Harry had not mentioned his intentions either to James Starr or to the old overman. Jack had been discreet enough to say nothing.

Harry had provided himself with a rope about 200 feet long. It was not particularly thick, but very strong—sufficiently so to sustain his weight. His friends were to let him down into the gulf, and his pulling the cord was to be the signal to withdraw him.

The opening into this shaft or well was twelve feet wide. A beam was thrown across like a bridge, so that the cord passing over it should hang down the center of the opening, and save Harry from striking against the sides in his descent.

He was ready.

"Are you still determined to explore this abyss?" whispered Jack Ryan.

"Yes, I am, Jack."

The cord was fastened round Harry's thighs and under his arms, to keep him from rocking. Thus supported, he was free to use both his hands. A safety-lamp hung at his belt, also a large, strong knife in a leather sheath.

Harry advanced to the middle of the beam, around which the cord was passed. Then his friends began to let him down, and he slowly sank into the pit. As the rope caused him to swing gently round and round, the light of his lamp fell in turns on all points of the side walls, so that he was able to examine them carefully. These walls consisted of pit coal, and so smooth that it would be impossible to ascend them.

Harry calculated that he was going down at the rate of about a foot per second, so that he had time to look about him, and be ready for any event.

During two minutes—that is to say, to the depth of about 120 feet, the descent continued without any incident.

No lateral gallery opened from the side walls of the pit, which was gradually narrowing into the shape of a funnel. But Harry began to feel a fresher air rising from beneath, whence he concluded that the bottom of the pit communicated with a gallery of some description in the lowest part of the mine.

The cord continued to unwind. Darkness and silence were complete. If any living being whatever had sought refuge in the deep and mysterious abyss, he had either left it, or, if there, by no movement did he in the slightest way betray his presence.

Harry, becoming more suspicious the lower he got, now drew his knife and held it in his right hand. At a depth of 180 feet, his feet touched the lower point and the cord slackened and unwound no further.

Harry breathed more freely for a moment. One of the fears he entertained had been that, during his descent, the cord might be cut above him, but he had seen no projection from the walls behind which anyone could have been concealed.

The bottom of the abyss was quite dry. Harry, taking the lamp from his belt, walked round the place, and perceived he had been right in his conjectures.

An extremely narrow passage led aside out of the pit. He had to stoop to look into it, and only by creeping could it be followed; but as he wanted to see in which direction it led, and whether another abyss opened from it, he lay down on the ground and began to enter it on hands and knees.

An obstacle speedily arrested his progress. He fancied he could perceive by touching it, that a human body lay across the passage. A sudden thrill of horror and surprise made him hastily draw back, but he again advanced and felt more carefully.

His senses had not deceived him; a body did indeed lie there; and he soon ascertained that, although icy cold at the extremities, there was some vital heat remaining. In less time than it takes to tell it, Harry had drawn the body from the recess to the bottom of the shaft, and, seizing his lamp, he cast its lights on what he had found, exclaiming immediately, "Why, it is a child!"

The child still breathed, but so very feebly that Harry expected it to cease every instant. Not a moment was to be lost; he must carry this poor little creature out of the pit, and take it home to his mother as quickly as he could. He eagerly fastened the cord round his waist, stuck on his lamp, clasped the child to his breast with his left arm, and, keeping his right hand free to hold the knife, he gave the signal agreed on, to have the rope pulled up.

It tightened at once; he began the ascent. Harry looked around him with redoubled care, for more than his own life was now in danger.

For a few minutes all went well, no accident seemed to threaten him, when suddenly he heard the sound of a great rush of air from beneath; and, looking down, he could dimly perceive through the gloom a broad mass arising until it passed him, striking him as it went by.

It was an enormous bird—of what sort he could not see; it flew upwards on mighty wings, then paused, hovered, and dashed fiercely down upon Harry, who could only wield his knife in one hand. He defended himself and the child as well as he could, but the ferocious bird seemed to aim all its blows at him alone. Afraid of cutting the cord, he could not strike it as he wished, and the struggle was prolonged, while Harry shouted with all his might in hopes of making his comrades hear.

He soon knew they did, for they pulled the rope up faster; a distance of about eighty feet remained to be got over. The bird ceased its direct attack, but increased the horror and danger of his situation by rushing at the cord, clinging to it just out of his reach, and endeavoring, by pecking furiously, to cut it.

Harry felt overcome with terrible dread. One strand of the rope gave way, and it made them sink a little.

A shriek of despair escaped his lips.

A second strand was divided, and the double burden now hung suspended by only half the cord.

Harry dropped his knife, and by a superhuman effort succeeded, at the moment the rope was giving way, in catching hold of it with his right hand above the cut made by the beak of the bird. But, powerfully as he held it in his iron grasp, he could feel it gradually slipping through his fingers.

He might have caught it, and held on with both hands by sacrificing the life of the child he supported in his left arm. The idea crossed him, but was banished in an instant, although he believed himself quite unable to hold out until drawn to the surface. For a second he closed his eyes, believing they were about to plunge back into the abyss.

He looked up once more; the huge bird had disappeared; his hand was at the very extremity of the broken rope—when, just as his convulsive grasp was failing, he was seized by the men, and with the child was placed on the level ground.

The fearful strain of anxiety removed, a reaction took place, and Harry fell fainting into the arms of his friends.

***

# CHAPTER XII

# NELL ADOPTED

A couple of hours later, Harry still unconscious, and the child in a very feeble state, were brought to the cottage by Jack Ryan and his companions. The old overman listened to the account of their adventures, while Madge attended with the utmost care to the wants of her son, and of the poor creature whom he had rescued from the pit.

Harry imagined her a mere child, but she was a maiden of the age of fifteen or sixteen years.

She gazed at them with vague and wondering eyes; and the thin face, drawn by suffering, the pallid complexion, which light could never have tinged, and the fragile, slender figure, gave her an appearance at once singular and attractive. Jack Ryan declared that she seemed to him to be an uncommonly interesting kind of ghost.

It must have been due to the strange and peculiar circumstances under which her life hitherto had been led, that she scarcely seemed to belong to the human race. Her countenance was of a very uncommon cast, and her eyes, hardly able to bear the lamp-light in the cottage, glanced around in a confused and puzzled way, as if all were new to them.

As this singular being reclined on Madge's bed and awoke to consciousness, as from a long sleep, the old Scotchwoman began to question her a little.

"What do they call you, my dear?" said she.

"Nell," replied the girl.

"Do you feel anything the matter with you, Nell?"

"I am hungry. I have eaten nothing since—since—"

Nell uttered these few words like one unused to speak much. They were in the Gaelic language, which was often spoken by Simon and his family. Madge immediately brought her some food; she was evidently famished. It was impossible to say how long she might have been in that pit.

"How many days had you been down there, dearie?" inquired Madge.

Nell made no answer; she seemed not to understand the question.

"How many days, do you think?"

"Days?" repeated Nell, as though the word had no meaning for her, and she shook her head to signify entire want of comprehension.

Madge took her hand, and stroked it caressingly. "How old are you, my lassie?" she asked, smiling kindly at her.

Nell shook her head again.

"Yes, yes," continued Madge, "how many years old?"

"Years?" replied Nell. She seemed to understand that word no better than days! Simon, Harry, Jack, and the rest, looked on with an air of mingled compassion, wonder, and sympathy. The state of this poor thing, clothed in a miserable garment of coarse woolen stuff, seemed to impress them painfully.

Harry, more than all the rest, seemed attracted by the very peculiarity of this poor stranger. He drew near, took Nell's hand from his mother, and looked directly at her, while something like a smile curved her lip. "Nell," he said, "Nell, away down there—in the mine—were you all alone?"

"Alone! alone!" cried the girl, raising herself hastily. Her features expressed terror; her eyes, which had appeared to soften as Harry looked at her, became quite wild again. "Alone!" repeated she, "alone!"—and she fell back on the bed, as though deprived of all strength.

"The poor bairn is too weak to speak to us," said Madge, when she had adjusted the pillows. "After a good rest, and a little more food, she will be stronger. Come away, Simon and Harry, and all the rest of you, and let her go to sleep." So Nell was left alone, and in a very few minutes slept profoundly.

This event caused a great sensation, not only in the coal mines, but in Stirlingshire, and ultimately throughout the kingdom. The strangeness of the story was exaggerated; the affair could not have made more commotion had they found the girl enclosed in the solid rock, like one of those antediluvian creatures who have occasionally been released by a stroke of the pickax from their stony prison. Nell became a fashionable wonder without knowing it. Superstitious folks made her story a new subject for legendary marvels, and were inclined to think, as Jack Ryan told Harry, that Nell was the spirit of the mines.

"Be it so, Jack," said the young man; "but at any rate she is the good spirit. It can have been none but she who brought us bread and water when we were shut up down there; and as to the bad spirit, who must still be in the mine, we'll catch him some day."

Of course James Starr had been at once informed of all this, and came, as soon as the young girl had sufficiently recovered her strength, to see her, and endeavor to question her carefully.

She appeared ignorant of nearly everything relating to life, and, although evidently intelligent, was wanting in many elementary ideas, such as time, for instance. She had never been used to its division, and the words signifying hours, days, months, and years were unknown to her.

Her eyes, accustomed to the night, were pained by the glare of the electric discs; but in the dark her sight was wonderfully keen, the pupil dilated in a remarkable manner, and she could see where to others there appeared profound obscurity. It was certain that her brain had never received any impression of the outer world, that her eyes had never looked beyond the mine, and that these somber depths had been all the world to her.

The poor girl probably knew not that there were a sun and stars, towns and counties, a mighty universe composed of myriads of worlds.

But until she comprehended the significance of words at present conveying no precise meaning to her, it was impossible to ascertain what she knew.

As to whether or not Nell had lived alone in the recesses of New Aberfoyle, James Starr was obliged to remain uncertain; indeed, any allusion to the subject excited evident alarm in the mind of this strange girl. Either Nell could not or would not reply to questions, but that some secret existed in connection with the place, which she could have explained, was manifest.

"Should you like to stay with us? Should you like to go back to where we found you?" asked James Starr.

"Oh, yes!" exclaimed the maiden, in answer to his first question; but a cry of terror was all she seemed able to say to the second.

James Starr, as well as Simon and Harry Ford, could not help feeling a certain amount of uneasiness with regard to this persistent silence. They found it impossible to forget all that had appeared so inexplicable at the time they made the discovery of the coal mine; and although that was three years ago, and nothing new had happened, they always expected some fresh attack on the part of the invisible enemy.

They resolved to explore the mysterious well, and did so, well armed and in considerable numbers. But nothing suspicious was to be seen; the shaft communicated with lower stages of the crypt, hollowed out in the carboniferous bed.

Many a time did James Starr, Simon, and Harry talk over these things. If one or more malevolent beings were concealed in the coal-pit, and there concocted mischief, Nell surely could have warned them of it, yet she said nothing. The slightest allusion to her past life brought on such fits of violent emotion, that it was judged best to avoid the subject for the present. Her secret would certainly escape her by-and-by.

By the time Nell had been a fortnight in the cottage, she had become a most intelligent and zealous assistant to old Madge. It was clear that she instinctively felt she should remain in the dwelling where she had been so charitably received, and perhaps never dreamt of quitting it.

This family was all in all to her, and to the good folks themselves Nell had seemed an adopted child from the moment when she first came beneath their roof. Nell was in truth a charming creature; her new mode of existence added to her beauty, for these were no doubt the first happy days of her life, and her heart was full of gratitude towards those to whom she owed them. Madge felt towards her as a mother would; the old woman doted upon her; in short, she was beloved by everybody. Jack Ryan only regretted one thing, which was that he had not saved her himself. Friend Jack often came to the cottage. He sang, and Nell, who had never heard singing before, admired it greatly; but anyone might see that she preferred to Jack's songs the graver conversation of Harry, from whom by degrees she learnt truths concerning the outer world, of which hitherto she had known nothing.

It must be said that, since Nell had appeared in her own person, Jack Ryan had been obliged to admit that his belief in hobgoblins was in a measure weakened. A couple of months later his credulity experienced a further shock. About that time Harry unexpectedly made a discovery which, in part at least, accounted for the apparition of the fire-maidens among the ruins of Dundonald Castle at Irvine.

During several days he had been engaged in exploring the remote galleries of the prodigious excavation towards the south. At last he scrambled with difficulty up a narrow passage which branched off through the upper rock. To his great astonishment, he suddenly found himself in the open air. The passage, after ascending obliquely to the surface of the ground, led out directly among the ruins of Dundonald Castle.

There was, therefore, a communication between New Aberfoyle and the hills crowned by this ancient castle. The upper entrance to this gallery, being completely concealed by stones and brushwood, was invisible from without; at the time of their search, therefore, the magistrates had been able to discover nothing.

A few days afterwards, James Starr, guided by Harry, came himself to inspect this curious natural opening into the coal mine. "Well," said he, "here is enough to convince the most superstitious among us. Farewell to all their brownies, goblins, and fire-maidens now!"

"I hardly think, Mr. Starr, we ought to congratulate ourselves," replied Harry. "Whatever it is we have instead of these things, it can't be better, and may be worse than they are."

"That's true, Harry," said the engineer; "but what's to be done? It is plain that, whatever the beings are who hide in the mine, they reach the surface of the earth by this passage. No doubt it was the light of torches waved by them during that dark and stormy night which attracted the *Motala* towards the rocky coast, and like the wreckers of former days, they would have plundered the unfortunate vessel, had it not been for Jack Ryan and his friends. Anyhow, so far it is evident, and here is the mouth of the den. As to its occupants, the question is—Are they here still?"

"I say yes; because Nell trembles when we mention them—yes, because Nell will not, or dare not, speak about them," answered Harry in a tone of decision.

Harry was surely in the right. Had these mysterious denizens of the pit abandoned it, or ceased to visit the spot, what reason could the girl have had for keeping silence?

James Starr could not rest till he had penetrated this mystery. He foresaw that the whole future of the new excavations must depend upon it. Renewed and strict precautions were therefore taken. The authorities were informed of the discovery of the entrance. Watchers were placed among the ruins of the castle. Harry himself lay hid for several nights in the thickets of brushwood which clothed the hill-side.

Nothing was discovered—no human being emerged from the opening. So most people came to the conclusion that the villains had been finally dislodged from the mine, and that, as to Nell, they must suppose her to be dead at the bottom of the shaft where they had left her.

While it remained unworked, the mine had been a safe enough place of refuge, secure from all search or pursuit. But now, circumstances being altered, it became difficult to conceal this lurking-place, and it might reasonably be hoped they were gone, and that nothing for the future was to be dreaded from them.

James Starr, however, could not feel sure about it; neither could Harry be satisfied on the subject, often repeating, "Nell has clearly been mixed up with all this secret business. If she had nothing more to fear, why should she keep silence? It cannot be doubted that she is happy with us. She likes us all—she adores my mother. Her absolute silence as to her former life, when by speaking out she might benefit us, proves to me that some awful secret, which she dares not reveal, weighs on her mind. It may also be that she believes it better for us, as well as for herself, that she should remain mute in a way otherwise so unaccountable."

In consequence of these opinions, it was agreed by common consent to avoid all allusion to the maiden's former mode of life. One day, however, Harry was led to make known to Nell what James Starr, his father, mother, and himself believed they owed to her interference.

It was a fête-day. The miners made holiday on the surface of the county of Stirling as well as in its subterraneous domains. Parties of holiday-makers were moving about in all directions. Songs resounded in many places beneath the sonorous vaults of New Aberfoyle. Harry and Nell left the cottage, and slowly walked along the left bank of Loch Malcolm.

Then the electric brilliance darted less vividly, and the rays were interrupted with fantastic effect by the sharp angles of the picturesque rocks which supported the dome. This imperfect light suited Nell, to whose eyes a glare was very unpleasant.

"Nell," said Harry, "your eyes are not fit for daylight yet, and could not bear the brightness of the sun."

"Indeed they could not," replied the girl; "if the sun is such as you describe it to me, Harry."

"I cannot by any words, Nell, give you an idea either of his splendor or of the beauty of that universe which your eyes have never beheld. But tell me, is it really possible that, since the day when you were born in the depths of the coal mine, you never once have been up to the surface of the earth?"

"Never once, Harry," said she; "I do not believe that, even as an infant, my father or mother ever carried me thither. I am sure I should have retained some impression of the open air if they had."

"I believe you would," answered Harry. "Long ago, Nell, many children used to live altogether in the mine; communication was then difficult, and I have met with more than one young person, quite as ignorant as you are of things above-ground. But now the railway through our great tunnel takes us in a few minutes to the upper regions of our country. I long, Nell, to hear you say, 'Come, Harry, my eyes can bear daylight, and I want to see the sun! I want to look upon the works of the Almighty.'"

"I shall soon say so, Harry, I hope," replied the girl; "I shall soon go with you to the world above; and yet—"

"What are you going to say, Nell?" hastily cried Harry; "can you possibly regret having quitted that gloomy abyss in which you spent your early years, and whence we drew you half dead?"

"No, Harry," answered Nell; "I was only thinking that darkness is beautiful as well as light. If you but knew what eyes accustomed to its depth can see! Shades flit by, which one longs to follow; circles mingle and intertwine, and one could gaze on them forever; black hollows, full of indefinite gleams of radiance, lie deep at the bottom of the mine. And then the voice-like sounds! Ah, Harry! one must have lived down there to understand what I feel, what I can never express."

"And were you not afraid, Nell, all alone there?"

"It was just when I was alone that I was not afraid."

Nell's voice altered slightly as she said these words; however, Harry thought he might press the subject a little further, so he said, "But one might be easily lost in these great galleries, Nell. Were you not afraid of losing your way?"

"Oh, no, Harry; for a long time I had known every turn of the new mine."

"Did you never leave it?"

"Yes, now and then," answered the girl with a little hesitation; "sometimes I have been as far as the old mine of Aberfoyle."

"So you knew our old cottage?"

"The cottage! oh, yes; but the people who lived there I only saw at a great distance."

"They were my father and mother," said Harry; "and I was there too; we have always lived there—we never would give up the old dwelling."

"Perhaps it would have been better for you if you had," murmured the maiden.

"Why so, Nell? Was it not just because we were obstinately resolved to remain that we ended by discovering the new vein of coal? And did not that discovery lead to the happy result of providing work for a large population, and restoring them to ease and comfort? and did it not enable us to find you, Nell, to save your life, and give you the love of all our hearts?"

"Ah, yes, for me indeed it is well, whatever may happen," replied Nell earnestly; "for others—who can tell?"

"What do you mean?"

"Oh, nothing—nothing. But it used to be very dangerous at that time to go into the new cutting—yes, very dangerous indeed, Harry! Once some rash people made their way into these chasms. They got a long, long way; they were lost!"

"They were lost?" said Harry, looking at her.

"Yes, lost!" repeated Nell in a trembling voice. "They could not find their way out."

"And there," cried Harry, "they were imprisoned during eight long days! They were at the point of death, Nell; and, but for a kind and charitable being—an angel perhaps—sent by God to help them, who secretly brought them a little food; but for a mysterious guide, who afterwards led to them their deliverers, they never would have escaped from that living tomb!"

"And how do you know about that?" demanded the girl.

"Because those men were James Starr, my father, and myself, Nell!"

Nell looked up hastily, seized the young man's hand, and gazed so fixedly into his eyes that his feelings were stirred to their depths. "You were there?" at last she uttered.

"I was indeed," said Harry, after a pause, "and she to whom we owe our lives can have been none other than yourself, Nell!"

Nell hid her face in her hands without speaking. Harry had never seen her so much affected.

"Those who saved your life, Nell," added he in a voice tremulous with emotion, "already owed theirs to you; do you think they will ever forget it?"

***

## CHAPTER XIII

## ON THE REVOLVING LADDER

The mining operations at New Aberfoyle continued to be carried on very successfully. As a matter of course, the engineer, James Starr, as well as Simon Ford, the discoverers of this rich carboniferous region, shared largely in the profits.

In time Harry became a partner. But he never thought of quitting the cottage. He took his father's place as overman, and diligently superintended the works of this colony of miners. Jack Ryan was proud and delighted at the good fortune which had befallen his comrade. He himself was getting on very well also.

They frequently met, either at the cottage or at the works in the pit. Jack did not fail to remark the sentiments entertained by Harry towards Nell. Harry would not confess to them; but Jack only laughed at him when he shook his head and tried to deny any special interest in her.

It must be noted that Jack Ryan had the greatest possible wish to be of the party when Nell should pay her first visit to the upper surface of the county of Stirling. He wished to see her wonder and admiration on first beholding the yet unknown face of Nature. He very much hoped that Harry would take him with them when the excursion was made. As yet, however, the latter had made no proposal of the kind to him, which caused him to feel a little uneasy as to his intentions.

One morning Jack Ryan was descending through a shaft which led from the surface to the lower regions of the pit. He did so by means of one of those ladders which, continually revolving by machinery, enabled persons to ascend and descend without fatigue.

This apparatus had lowered him about a hundred and fifty feet, when at a narrow landing-place he perceived Harry, who was coming up to his labors for the day.

"Well met, my friend!" cried Jack, recognizing his comrade by the light of the electric lamps.

"Ah, Jack!" replied Harry, "I am glad to see you. I've got something to propose."

"I can listen to nothing till you tell me how Nell is," interrupted Jack Ryan.

"Nell is all right, Jack—so much so, in fact, that I hope in a month or six weeks—"

"To marry her, Harry?"

"Jack, you don't know what you are talking about!"

"Ah, that's very likely; but I know quite well what I shall do."

"What will you do?"

"Marry her myself, if you don't; so look sharp," laughed Jack. "By Saint Mungo! I think an immense deal of bonny Nell! A fine young creature like that, who has been brought up in the mine, is just the very wife for a miner. She is an orphan—so am I; and if you don't care much for her, and if she will have me—"

Harry looked gravely at Jack, and let him talk on without trying to stop him. "Don't you begin to feel jealous, Harry?" asked Jack in a more serious tone.

"Not at all," answered Harry quietly.

"But if you don't marry Nell yourself, you surely can't expect her to remain a spinster?"

"I expect nothing," said Harry.

A movement of the ladder machinery now gave the two friends the opportunity—one to go up, the other down the shaft. However, they remained where they were.

"Harry," quoth Jack, "do you think I spoke in earnest just now about Nell?"

"No, that I don't, Jack."

"Well, but now I will!"

"You? speak in earnest?"

"My good fellow, I can tell you I am quite capable of giving a friend a bit of advice."

"Let's hear, then, Jack!"

"Well, look here! You love Nell as heartily as she deserves. Old Simon, your father, and old Madge, your mother, both love her as if she were their daughter. Why don't you make her so in reality? Why don't you marry her?"

"Come, Jack," said Harry, "you are running on as if you knew how Nell felt on the subject."

"Everybody knows that," replied Jack, "and therefore it is impossible to make you jealous of any of us. But here goes the ladder again—I'm off!"

"Stop a minute, Jack!" cried Harry, detaining his companion, who was stepping onto the moving staircase.

"I say! you seem to mean me to take up my quarters here altogether!"

"Do be serious and listen, Jack! I want to speak in earnest myself now."

"Well, I'll listen till the ladder moves again, not a minute longer."

"Jack," resumed Harry, "I need not pretend that I do not love Nell; I wish above all things to make her my wife."

"That's all right!"

"But for the present I have scruples of conscience as to asking her to make me a promise which would be irrevocable."

"What can you mean, Harry?"

"I mean just this—that, it being certain Nell has never been outside this coal mine in the very depths of which she was born, it stands to reason that she knows nothing, and can comprehend nothing of what exists beyond it. Her eyes—yes, and perhaps also her heart—have everything yet to learn. Who can tell what her thoughts will be, when perfectly new impressions shall be made upon her mind? As yet she knows nothing of the world, and to me it would seem like deceiving her, if I led her to decide in ignorance, upon choosing to remain all her life in the coal mine. Do you understand me, Jack?"

"Hem!—yes—pretty well. What I understand best is that you are going to make me miss another turn of the ladder."

"Jack," replied Harry gravely, "if this machinery were to stop altogether, if this landing-place were to fall beneath our feet, you must and shall hear what I have to say."

"Well done, Harry! that's how I like to be spoken to! Let's settle, then, that, before you marry Nell, she shall go to school in Auld Reekie."

"No indeed, Jack; I am perfectly able myself to educate the person who is to be my wife."

"Sure that will be a great deal better, Harry!"

"But, first of all," resumed Harry, "I wish that Nell should gain a real knowledge of the upper world. To illustrate my meaning, Jack, suppose you were in love with a blind girl, and someone said to you, 'In a month's time her sight will be restored,' would you not wait till after she was cured, to marry her?"

"Faith, to be sure I would!" exclaimed Jack.

"Well, Jack, Nell is at present blind; and before she marries me, I wish her to see what I am, and what the life really is to which she would bind herself. In short, she must have daylight let in upon the subject!"

"Well said, Harry! Very well said indeed!" cried Jack. "Now I see what you are driving at. And when may we expect the operation to come off?"

"In a month, Jack," replied Harry. "Nell is getting used to the light of our reflectors. That is some preparation. In a month she will, I hope, have seen the earth and its wonders—the sky and its splendors. She will perceive that the limits of the universe are boundless."

But while Harry was thus giving the rein to his imagination, Jack Ryan, quitting the platform, had leaped on the step of the moving machinery.

"Hullo, Jack! Where are you?"

"Far beneath you," laughed the merry fellow. "While you soar to the heights, I plunge into the depths."

"Fare ye well. Jack!" returned Harry, himself laying hold of the rising ladder; "mind you say nothing about what I have been telling you."

"Not a word," shouted Jack, "but I make one condition."

"What is that?"

"That I may be one of the party when Nell's first excursion to the face of the earth comes off!"

"So you shall, Jack, I promise you!"

A fresh throb of the machinery placed a yet more considerable distance between the friends. Their voices sounded faintly to each other. Harry, however, could still hear Jack shouting:

"I say! do you know what Nell will like better than either sun, moon, or stars, after she's seen the whole of them?"

"No, Jack!"

"Why, you yourself, old fellow! still you! always you!" And Jack's voice died away in a prolonged "Hurrah!"

Harry, after this, applied himself diligently, during all his spare time, to the work of Nell's education. He taught her to read and to write, and such rapid progress did she make, it might have been said that she learnt by instinct. Never did keen intelligence more quickly triumph over utter ignorance. It was the wonder of all beholders.

Simon and Madge became every day more and more attached to their adopted child, whose former history continued to puzzle them a good deal. They plainly saw the nature of Harry's feelings towards her, and were far from displeased thereat. They recollected that Simon had said to the engineer on his first visit to the old cottage, "How can our son ever think of marrying? Where could a wife possibly be found suitable for a lad whose whole life must be passed in the depths of a coal mine?"

Well! now it seemed as if the most desirable companion in the world had been led to him by Providence. Was not this like a blessing direct from Heaven? So the old man made up his mind that, if the wedding did take place, the miners of New Aberfoyle should have a merry-making at Coal Town, which they would never during their lives forget. Simon Ford little knew what he was saying!

It must be remarked that another person wished for this union of Harry and Nell as much as Simon did—and that was James Starr, the engineer. Of course he was really interested in the happiness of the two young people. But another motive, connected with wider interests, influenced him to desire it.

It has been said that James Starr continued to entertain a certain amount of apprehension, although for the present nothing appeared to justify it. Yet that which had been might again be. This mystery about the new cutting—Nell was evidently the only person acquainted with it. Now, if fresh dangers were in store for the miners of Aberfoyle, how were they possibly to be guarded against, without so much as knowing the cause of them?

"Nell has persisted in keeping silence," said James Starr very often, "but what she has concealed from others, she will not long hide from her husband. Any danger would be danger to Harry as well as to the rest of us. Therefore, a marriage which brings happiness to the lovers, and safety to their friends, will be a good marriage, if ever there is such a thing here below."

Thus, not illogically, reasoned James Starr. He communicated his ideas to old Simon, who decidedly appreciated them. Nothing, then, appeared to stand in the way of the match. What, in fact, was there to prevent it? They loved each other; the parents desired nothing better for their son. Harry's comrades envied his good fortune, but freely acknowledged that he deserved it. The maiden depended on no one else, and had but to give the consent of her own heart.

Why, then, if there were none to place obstacles in the way of this union—why, as night came on, and, the labors of the day being over, the electric lights in the mine were extinguished, and all the inhabitants of Coal Town at rest within their dwellings—why did a mysterious form always emerge from the gloomier recesses of New Aberfoyle, and silently glide through the darkness?

What instinct guided this phantom with ease through passages so narrow as to appear to be impracticable?

Why should the strange being, with eyes flashing through the deepest darkness, come cautiously creeping along the shores of Lake Malcolm? Why so directly make his way towards Simon's cottage, yet so carefully as hitherto to avoid notice? Why, bending towards the windows, did he strive to catch, by listening, some fragment of the conversation within the closed shutters?

And, on catching a few words, why did he shake his fist with a menacing gesture towards the calm abode, while from between his set teeth issued these words in muttered fury, "She and he? Never! never!"

***

## CHAPTER XIV

## A SUNRISE

A month after this, on the evening of the 20th of August, Simon Ford and Madge took leave, with all manner of good wishes, of four tourists, who were setting forth from the cottage.

James Starr, Harry, and Jack Ryan were about to lead Nell's steps over yet untrodden paths, and to show her the glories of nature by a light to which she was as yet a stranger. The excursion was to last for two days. James Starr, as well as Harry, considered that during these eight and forty hours spent above ground, the maiden would be able to see everything of which she must have remained ignorant in the gloomy pit; all the varied aspects of the globe, towns, plains, mountains, rivers, lakes, gulfs, and seas would pass, panorama-like, before her eyes.

In that part of Scotland lying between Edinburgh and Glasgow, nature would seem to have collected and set forth specimens of every one of these terrestrial beauties. As to the heavens, they would be spread abroad as over the whole earth, with their changeful clouds, serene or veiled moon, their radiant sun, and clustering stars. The expedition had been planned so as to combine a view of all these things.

Simon and Madge would have been glad to go with Nell; but they never left their cottage willingly, and could not make up their minds to quit their subterranean home for a single day.

James Starr went as an observer and philosopher, curious to note, from a psychological point of view, the novel impressions made upon Nell; perhaps also with some hope of detecting a clue to the mysterious events connected with her childhood. Harry, with a little trepidation, asked himself whether it was not possible that this rapid initiation into the things of the exterior world would change the maiden he had known and loved hitherto into quite a different girl. As for Jack Ryan, he was as joyous as a lark rising in the first beams of the sun. He only trusted that his gayety would prove contagious, and enliven his traveling companions, thus rewarding them for letting him join them. Nell was pensive and silent.

James Starr had decided, very sensibly, to set off in the evening. It would be very much better for the girl to pass gradually from the darkness of night to the full light of day; and that would in this way be managed, since between midnight and noon she would experience the successive phases of shade and sunshine, to which her sight had to get accustomed.

Just as they left the cottage, Nell took Harry's hand saying, "Harry, is it really necessary for me to leave the mine at all, even for these few days?"

"Yes, it is, Nell," replied the young man. "It is needful for both of us."

"But, Harry," resumed Nell, "ever since you found me, I have been as happy as I can possibly be. You have been teaching me. Why is that not enough? What am I going up there for?"

Harry looked at her in silence. Nell was giving utterance to nearly his own thoughts.

"My child," said James Starr, "I can well understand the hesitation you feel; but it will be good for you to go with us. Those who love you are taking you, and they will bring you back again. Afterwards you will be free, if you wish it, to continue your life in the coal mine, like old Simon, and Madge, and Harry. But at least you ought to be able to compare what you give up with what you choose, then decide freely. Come!"

"Come, dear Nell!" cried Harry.

"Harry, I am willing to follow you," replied the maiden. At nine o'clock the last train through the tunnel started to convey Nell and her companions to the surface of the earth. Twenty minutes later they alighted on the platform where the branch line to New Aberfoyle joins the railway from Dumbarton to Stirling.

The night was already dark. From the horizon to the zenith, light vapory clouds hurried through the upper air, driven by a refreshing northwesterly breeze. The day had been lovely; the night promised to be so likewise.

On reaching Stirling, Nell and her friends, quitting the train, left the station immediately. Just before them, between high trees, they could see a road which led to the banks of the river Forth.

The first physical impression on the girl was the purity of the air inhaled eagerly by her lungs.

"Breathe it freely, Nell," said James Starr; "it is fragrant with all the scents of the open country."

"What is all that smoke passing over our heads?" inquired Nell.

"Those are clouds," answered Harry, "blown along by the westerly wind."

"Ah!" said Nell, "how I should like to feel myself carried along in that silent whirl! And what are those shining sparks which glance here and there between rents in the clouds?"

"Those are the stars I have told you about, Nell. So many suns they are, so many centers of worlds like our own, most likely."

The constellations became more clearly visible as the wind cleared the clouds from the deep blue of the firmament. Nell gazed upon the myriad stars which sparkled overhead. "But how is it," she said at length, "that if these are suns, my eyes can endure their brightness?"

"My child," replied James Starr, "they are indeed suns, but suns at an enormous distance. The nearest of these millions of stars, whose rays can reach us, is Vega, that star in Lyra which you observe near the zenith, and that is fifty thousand millions of leagues distant. Its brightness, therefore, cannot affect your vision. But our own sun, which will rise to-morrow, is only distant thirty-eight millions of leagues, and no human eye can gaze fixedly upon that, for it is brighter than the blaze of any furnace. But come, Nell, come!"

They pursued their way, James Starr leading the maiden, Harry walking by her side, while Jack Ryan roamed about like a young dog, impatient of the slow pace of his masters. The road was lonely. Nell kept looking at the great trees, whose branches, waving in the wind, made them seem to her like giants gesticulating wildly. The sound of the breeze in the tree-tops, the deep silence during a lull, the distant line of the horizon, which could be discerned when the road passed over open levels—all these things filled her with new sensations, and left lasting impressions on her mind.

After some time she ceased to ask questions, and her companions respected her silence, not wishing to influence by any words of theirs the girl's highly sensitive imagination, but preferring to allow ideas to arise spontaneously in her soul.

At about half past eleven o'clock, they gained the banks of the river Forth. There a boat, chartered by James Starr, awaited them. In a few hours it would convey them all to Granton. Nell looked at the clear water which flowed up to her feet, as the waves broke gently on the beach, reflecting the starlight. "Is this a lake?" said she.

"No," replied Harry, "it is a great river flowing towards the sea, and soon opening so widely as to resemble a gulf. Taste a little of the water in the hollow of your hand, Nell, and you will perceive that it is not sweet like the waters of Lake Malcolm."

The maiden bent towards the stream, and, raising a little water to her lips, "This is quite salt," said she.

"Yes, the tide is full; the sea water flows up the river as far as this," answered Harry.

"Oh, Harry! Harry!" exclaimed the maiden, "what can that red glow on the horizon be? Is it a forest on fire?"

"No, it is the rising moon, Nell."

"To be sure, that's the moon," cried Jack Ryan, "a fine big silver plate, which the spirits of air hand round and round the sky to collect the stars in, like money."

"Why, Jack," said the engineer, laughing, "I had no idea you could strike out such bold comparisons!"

"Well, but, Mr. Starr, it is a just comparison. Don't you see the stars disappear as the moon passes on? so I suppose they drop into it."

"What you mean to say, Jack, is that the superior brilliancy of the moon eclipses that of stars of the sixth magnitude, therefore they vanish as she approaches."

"How beautiful all this is!" repeated Nell again and again, with her whole soul in her eyes. "But I thought the moon was round?"

"So she is, when 'full,'" said James Starr; "that means when she is just opposite to the sun. But to-night the moon is in the last quarter, shorn of her just proportions, and friend Jack's grand silver plate looks more like a barber's basin."

"Oh, Mr. Starr, what a base comparison!" he exclaimed, "I was just going to begin a sonnet to the moon, but your barber's basin has destroyed all chance of an inspiration."

Gradually the moon ascended the heavens. Before her light the lingering clouds fled away, while stars still sparkled in the west, beyond the influence of her radiance. Nell gazed in silence on the glorious spectacle. The soft silvery light was pleasant to her eyes, and her little trembling hand expressed to Harry, who clasped it, how deeply she was affected by the scene.

"Let us embark now," said James Starr. "We have to get to the top of Arthur's Seat before sunrise."

The boat was moored to a post on the bank. A boatman awaited them. Nell and her friends took their seats; the sail was spread; it quickly filled before the northwesterly breeze, and they sped on their way.

What a new sensation was this for the maiden! She had been rowed on the waters of Lake Malcolm; but the oar, handled ever so lightly by Harry, always betrayed effort on the part of the oarsman. Now, for the first time, Nell felt herself borne along with a gliding movement, like that of a balloon through the air. The water was smooth as a lake, and Nell reclined in the stern of the boat, enjoying its gentle rocking. Occasionally the effect of the moonlight on the waters was as though the boat sailed across a glittering silver field. Little wavelets rippled along the banks. It was enchanting.

At length Nell was overcome with drowsiness, her eyelids drooped, her head sank on Harry's shoulder—she slept. Harry, sorry that she should miss any of the beauties of this magnificent night, would have aroused her.

"Let her sleep!" said the engineer. "She will better enjoy the novelties of the day after a couple of hours' rest."

At two o'clock in the morning the boat reached Granton pier. Nell awoke. "Have I been asleep?" inquired she.

"No, my child," said James Starr. "You have been dreaming that you slept, that's all."

The night continued clear. The moon, riding in mid-heaven, diffused her rays on all sides. In the little port of Granton lay two or three fishing boats; they rocked gently on the waters of the Firth. The wind fell as the dawn approached. The atmosphere, clear of mists, promised one of those fine autumn days so delicious on the sea coast.

A soft, transparent film of vapor lay along the horizon; the first sunbeam would dissipate it; to the maiden it exhibited that aspect of the sea which seems to blend it with the sky. Her view was now enlarged, without producing the impression of the boundless infinity of ocean.

Harry taking Nell's hand, they followed James Starr and Jack Ryan as they traversed the deserted streets. To Nell, this suburb of the capital appeared only a collection of gloomy dark houses, just like Coal Town, only that the roof was higher, and gleamed with small lights.

She stepped lightly forward, and easily kept pace with Harry. "Are you not tired, Nell?" asked he, after half an hour's walking.

"No! my feet seem scarcely to touch the earth," returned she. "This sky above us seems so high up, I feel as if I could take wing and fly!"

"I say! keep hold of her!" cried Jack Ryan. "Our little Nell is too good to lose. I feel just as you describe though, myself, when I have not left the pit for a long time."

"It is when we no longer experience the oppressive effect of the vaulted rocky roof above Coal Town," said James Starr, "that the spacious firmament appears to us like a profound abyss into which we have, as it were, a desire to plunge. Is that what you feel, Nell?"

"Yes, Mr. Starr, it is exactly like that," said Nell. "It makes me feel giddy."

"Ah! you will soon get over that, Nell," said Harry. "You will get used to the outer world, and most likely forget all about our dark coal pit."

"No, Harry, never!" said Nell, and she put her hand over her eyes, as though she would recall the remembrance of everything she had lately quitted.

Between the silent dwellings of the city, the party passed along Leith Walk, and went round the Calton Hill, where stood, in the light of the gray dawn, the buildings of the Observatory and Nelson's Monument. By Regent's Bridge and the North Bridge they at last reached the lower extremity of the Canongate. The town still lay wrapt in slumber.

Nell pointed to a large building in the center of an open space, asking, "What great confused mass is that?"

"That confused mass, Nell, is the palace of the ancient kings of Scotland; that is Holyrood, where many a sad scene has been enacted! The historian can here invoke many a royal shade; from those of the early Scottish kings to that of the unhappy Mary Stuart, and the French king, Charles X. When day breaks, however, Nell, this palace will not look so very gloomy. Holyrood, with its four embattled towers, is not unlike some handsome country house. But let us pursue our way. There, just above the ancient Abbey of Holyrood, are the superb cliffs called Salisbury Crags. Arthur's Seat rises above them, and that is where we are going. From the summit of Arthur's Seat, Nell, your eyes shall behold the sun appear above the horizon seaward."

They entered the King's Park, then, gradually ascending they passed across the Queen's Drive, a splendid carriageway encircling the hill, which we owe to a few lines in one of Sir Walter Scott's romances.

Arthur's Seat is in truth only a hill, seven hundred and fifty feet high, which stands alone amid surrounding heights. In less than half an hour, by an easy winding path, James Starr and his party reached the crest of the crouching lion, which, seen from the west, Arthur's Seat so much resembles. There, all four seated themselves; and James Starr, ever ready with quotations from the great Scottish novelist, simply said, "Listen to what is written by Sir Walter Scott in the eighth chapter of the *Heart of Mid-Lothian*. 'If I were to choose a spot from which the rising or setting sun could be seen to the greatest possible advantage, it would be from this neighborhood.' Now watch, Nell! the sun will soon appear, and for the first time you will contemplate its splendor."

The maiden turned her eyes eastward. Harry, keeping close beside her, observed her with anxious interest. Would the first beams of day overpower her feelings? All remained quiet, even Jack Ryan. A faint streak of pale rose tinted the light vapors of the horizon. It was the first ray of light attacking the laggards of the night. Beneath the hill lay the silent city, massed confusedly in the twilight of dawn. Here and there lights twinkled among the houses of the old town. Westward rose many hill-tops, soon to be illuminated by tips of fire.

Now the distant horizon of the sea became more plainly visible. The scale of colors fell into the order of the solar. Every instant they increased in intensity, rose color became red, red became fiery, daylight dawned. Nell now glanced towards the city, of which the outlines became more distinct. Lofty monuments, slender steeples emerged from the gloom; a kind of ashy light was spread abroad. At length one solitary ray struck on the maiden's sight. It was that ray of green which, morning or evening, is reflected upwards from the sea when the horizon is clear.

An instant afterwards, Nell turned, and pointing towards a bright prominent point in the New Town, "Fire!" cried she.

"No, Nell, that is no fire," said Harry. "The sun has touched with gold the top of Sir Walter Scott's monument"—and, indeed, the extreme point of the monument blazed like the light of a pharos.

It was day—the sun arose—his disc seemed to glitter as though he indeed emerged from the waters of the sea. Appearing at first very large from the effects of refraction, he contracted as he rose and assumed the perfectly circular form. Soon no eye could endure the dazzling splendor; it was as though the mouth of a furnace was opened through the sky.

Nell closed her eyes, but her eyelids could not exclude the glare, and she pressed her fingers over them. Harry advised her to turn in the opposite direction. "Oh, no," said she, "my eyes must get used to look at what yours can bear to see!"

Even through her hands Nell perceived a rosy light, which became more white as the sun rose above the horizon. As her sight became accustomed to it, her eyelids were raised, and at length her eyes drank in the light of day.

The good child knelt down, exclaiming, "Oh Lord God! how beautiful is Thy creation!" Then she rose and looked around. At her feet extended the panorama of Edinburgh—the clear, distinct lines of streets in the New Town, and the irregular mass of houses, with their confused network of streets and lanes, which constitutes Auld Reekie, properly so called. Two heights commanded the entire city; Edinburgh Castle, crowning its huge basaltic rock, and the Calton Hill, bearing on its rounded summit, among other monuments, ruins built to represent those of the Parthenon at Athens.

Fine roadways led in all directions from the capital. To the north, the coast of the noble Firth of Forth was indented by a deep bay, in which could be seen the seaport town of Leith, between which and this Modern Athens of the north ran a street, straight as that leading to the Piraeus.

Beyond the wide Firth could be seen the soft outlines of the county of Fife, while beneath the spectator stretched the yellow sands of Portobello and Newhaven.

Nell could not speak. Her lips murmured a word or two indistinctly; she trembled, became giddy, her strength failed her; overcome by the purity of the air and the sublimity of the scene, she sank fainting into Harry's arms, who, watching her closely, was ready to support her.

The youthful maiden, hitherto entombed in the massive depths of the earth, had now obtained an idea of the universe—of the works both of God and of man. She had looked upon town and country, and beyond these, into the immensity of the sea, the infinity of the heavens.

***

## CHAPTER XV

## LOCH LOMOND AND LOCH KATRINE

Harry bore Nell carefully down the steeps of Arthur's Seat, and, accompanied by James Starr and Jack Ryan, they reached Lambert's Hotel. There a good breakfast restored their strength, and they began to make further plans for an excursion to the Highland lakes.

Nell was now refreshed, and able to look boldly forth into the sunshine, while her lungs with ease inhaled the free and healthful air. Her eyes learned gladly to know the harmonious varieties of color as they rested on the green trees, the azure skies, and all the endless shades of lovely flowers and plants.

The railway train, which they entered at the Waverley Station, conveyed Nell and her friends to Glasgow. There, from the new bridge across the Clyde, they watched the curious sea-like movement of the river. After a night's rest at Comrie's Royal Hotel, they betook themselves to the terminus of the Edinburgh and Glasgow Railway, from whence a train would rapidly carry them, by way of Dumbarton and Balloch, to the southern extremity of Loch Lomond.

"Now for the land of Rob Roy and Fergus MacIvor!—the scenery immortalized by the poetical descriptions of Walter Scott," exclaimed James Starr. "You don't know this country, Jack?"

"Only by its songs, Mr. Starr," replied Jack; "and judging by those, it must be grand."

"So it is, so it is!" cried the engineer, "and our dear Nell shall see it to the best advantage."

A steamboat, the *Sinclair* by name, awaited tourists about to make the excursion to the lakes. Nell and her companions went on board. The day had begun in brilliant sunshine, free from the British fogs which so often veil the skies.

The passengers were determined to lose none of the beauties of nature to be displayed during the thirty miles' voyage. Nell, seated between James Starr and Harry, drank in with every faculty the magnificent poetry with which lovely Scottish scenery is fraught. Numerous small isles and islets soon appeared, as though thickly sown on the bosom of the lake. The *Sinclair* steamed her way among them, while between them glimpses could be had of quiet valleys, or wild rocky gorges on the mainland.

"Nell," said James Starr, "every island here has its legend, perhaps its song, as well as the mountains which overshadow the lake. One may, without much exaggeration, say that the history of this country is written in gigantic characters of mountains and islands."

Nell listened, but these fighting stories made her sad. Why all that bloodshed on plains which to her seemed enormous, and where surely there must have been room for everybody?

The shores of the lake form a little harbor at Luss. Nell could for a moment catch sight of the old tower of its ancient castle. Then, the *Sinclair* turning northward, the tourists gazed upon Ben Lomond, towering nearly 3,000 feet above the level of the lake.

"Oh, what a noble mountain!" cried Nell; "what a view there must be from the top!"

"Yes, Nell," answered James Starr; "see how haughtily its peak rises from amidst the thicket of oaks, birches, and heather, which clothe the lower portion of the mountain! From thence one may see two-thirds of old Caledonia. This eastern side of the lake was the special abode of the clan McGregor. At no great distance, the struggles of the Jacobites and Hanoverians repeatedly dyed with blood these lonely glens. Over these scenes shines the pale moon, called in old ballads 'Macfarlane's lantern.' Among these rocks still echo the immortal names of Rob Roy and McGregor Campbell."

As the *Sinclair* advanced along the base of the mountain, the country became more and more abrupt in character. Trees were only scattered here and there; among them were the willows, slender wands of which were formerly used for hanging persons of low degree.

"To economize hemp," remarked James Starr.

The lake narrowed very much as it stretched northwards.

The steamer passed a few more islets, Inveruglas, Eilad-whow, where stand some ruins of a stronghold of the clan MacFarlane. At length the head of the loch was reached, and the *Sinclair* stopped at Inversnaid.

Leaving Loch Arklet on the left, a steep ascent led to the Inn of Stronachlacar, on the banks of Loch Katrine.

There, at the end of a light pier, floated a small steamboat, named, as a matter of course, the *Rob Roy*. The travelers immediately went on board; it was about to start. Loch Katrine is only ten miles in length; its width never exceeds two miles. The hills nearest it are full of a character peculiar to themselves.

"Here we are on this famous lake," said James Starr. "It has been compared to an eel on account of its length and windings: and justly so. They say that it never freezes. I know nothing about that, but what we want to think of is, that here are the scenes of the adventures in the *Lady of the Lake*. I believe, if friend Jack looked about him carefully, he might see, still gliding over the surface of the water, the shade of the slender form of sweet Ellen Douglas."

"To be sure, Mr. Starr," replied Jack; "why should I not? I may just as well see that pretty girl on the waters of Loch Katrine, as those ugly ghosts on Loch Malcolm in the coal pit."

It was by this time three o'clock in the afternoon. The less hilly shores of Loch Katrine westward extended like a picture framed between Ben An and Ben Venue. At the distance of half a mile was the entrance to the narrow bay, where was the landing-place for our tourists, who meant to return to Stirling by Callander.

Nell appeared completely worn out by the continued excitement of the day. A faint ejaculation was all she was able to utter in token of admiration as new objects of wonder or beauty met her gaze. She required some hours of rest, were it but to impress lastingly the recollection of all she had seen.

Her hand rested in Harry's, and, looking earnestly at her, he said, "Nell, dear Nell, we shall soon be home again in the gloomy region of the coal mine. Shall you not pine for what you have seen during these few hours spent in the glorious light of day?"

"No, Harry," replied the girl; "I shall like to think about it, but I am glad to go back with you to our dear old home."

"Nell!" said Harry, vainly attempting to steady his voice, "are you willing to be bound to me by the most sacred tie? Could you marry me, Nell?"

"Yes, Harry, I could, if you are sure that I am able to make you happy," answered the maiden, raising her innocent eyes to his.

Scarcely had she pronounced these words when an unaccountable phenomenon took place. The *Rob Roy*, still half a mile from land, experienced a violent shock. She suddenly grounded. No efforts of the engine could move her.

The cause of this accident was simply that Loch Katrine was all at once emptied, as though an enormous fissure had opened in its bed. In a few seconds it had the appearance of a sea beach at low water. Nearly the whole of its contents had vanished into the bosom of the earth.

"My friends!" exclaimed James Starr, as the cause of this marvel became suddenly clear to him, "God help New Aberfoyle!"

***

# CHAPTER XVI

# A FINAL THREAT

On that day, in the colliery of New Aberfoyle, work was going on in the usual regular way. In the distance could be heard the crash of great charges of dynamite, by which the carboniferous rocks were blasted. Here masses of coal were loosened by pick-ax and crowbar; there the perforating machines, with their harsh grating, bored through the masses of sandstone and schist.

Hollow, cavernous noises resounded on all sides. Draughts of air rushed along the ventilating galleries, and the wooden swing-doors slammed beneath their violent gusts. In the lower tunnels, trains of trucks kept passing along at the rate of fifteen miles an hour, while at their approach electric bells warned the workmen to cower down in the refuge places. Lifts went incessantly up and down, worked by powerful engines on the surface of the soil. Coal Town was throughout brilliantly lighted by the electric lamps at full power.

Mining operations were being carried on with the greatest activity; coal was being piled incessantly into the trucks, which went in hundreds to empty themselves into the corves at the bottom of the shaft. While parties of miners who had labored during the night were taking needful rest, the others worked without wasting an hour.

Old Simon Ford and Madge, having finished their dinner, were resting at the door of their cottage. Simon smoked a good pipe of tobacco, and from time to time the old couple spoke of Nell, of their boy, of Mr. Starr, and wondered how they liked their trip to the surface of the earth. Where would they be now? What would they be doing? How could they stay so long away from the mine without feeling homesick?

Just then a terrific roaring noise was heard. It was like the sound of a mighty cataract rushing down into the mine. The old people rose hastily. They perceived at once that the waters of Loch Malcolm were rising. A great wave, unfurling like a billow, swept up the bank and broke against the walls of the cottage. Simon caught his wife in his arms, and carried her to the upper part of their dwelling.

At the same moment, cries arose from all parts of Coal Town, which was threatened by a sudden inundation. The inhabitants fled for safety to the top of the schist rocks bordering the lake; terror spread in all directions; whole families in frantic haste rushed towards the tunnel in order to reach the upper regions of the pit.

It was feared that the sea had burst into the colliery, for its galleries and passages penetrated as far as the Caledonian Canal. In that case the entire excavation, vast as it was, would be completely flooded. Not a single inhabitant of New Aberfoyle would escape death.

But when the foremost fugitives reached the entrance to the tunnel, they encountered Simon Ford, who had quitted his cottage. "Stop, my friends, stop!" shouted the old man; "if our town is to be overwhelmed, the floods will rush faster than you can; no one can possibly escape. But see! the waters are rising no further! it appears to me the danger is over."

"And our comrades at the far end of the works—what about them?" cried some of the miners.

"There is nothing to fear for them," replied Simon; "they are working on a higher level than the bed of the loch."

It was soon evident that the old man was in the right. The sudden influx of water had rushed to the very lowest bed of the vast mine, and its only ultimate effect was to raise the level of Loch Malcolm a few feet. Coal Town was uninjured, and it was reasonable to hope that no one had perished in the flood of water which had descended to the depths of the mine never yet penetrated by the workmen.

Simon and his men could not decide whether this inundation was owing to the overflow of a subterranean sheet of water penetrating fissures in the solid rock, or to some underground torrent breaking through its worn bed, and precipitating itself to the lowest level of the mine. But that very same evening they knew what to think about it, for the local papers published an account of the marvelous phenomenon which Loch Katrine had exhibited.

The surprising news was soon after confirmed by the four travelers, who, returning with all possible speed to the cottage, learned with extreme satisfaction that no serious damage was done in New Aberfoyle.

The bed of Loch Katrine had fairly given way. The waters had suddenly broken through by an enormous fissure into the mine beneath. Of Sir Walter Scott's favorite loch there was not left enough to wet the pretty foot of the Lady of the Lake; all that remained was a pond of a few acres at the further extremity.

This singular event made a profound sensation in the country. It was a thing unheard of that a lake should in the space of a few minutes empty itself, and disappear into the bowels of the earth. There was nothing for it but to erase Loch Katrine from the map of Scotland until (by public subscription) it could be refilled, care being of course taken, in the first place, to stop the rent up tight. This catastrophe would have been the death of Sir Walter Scott, had he still been in the world.

The accident was explicable when it was ascertained that, between the bed of the lake and the vast cavity beneath, the geological strata had become reduced to a thin layer, incapable of longer sustaining the weight of water.

Now, although to most people this event seemed plainly due to natural causes, yet to James Starr and his friends, Simon and Harry Ford, the question constantly recurred, was it not rather to be attributed to malevolence? Uneasy suspicions continually harassed their minds. Was their evil genius about to renew his persecution of those who ventured to work this rich mine?

At the cottage, some days later, James Starr thus discussed the matter with the old man and his son: "Well, Simon," said he, "to my thinking we must class this circumstance with the others for which we still seek elucidation, although it is no doubt possible to explain it by natural causes."

"I am quite of your mind, Mr. James," replied Simon, "but take my advice, and say nothing about it; let us make all researches ourselves."

"Oh, I know the result of such research beforehand!" cried the engineer.

"And what will it be, then?"

"We shall find proofs of malevolence, but not the malefactor."

"But he exists! he is there! Where can he lie concealed? Is it possible to conceive that the most depraved human being could, single-handed, carry out an idea so infernal as that of bursting through the bed of a lake? I believe I shall end by thinking, like Jack Ryan, that the evil demon of the mine revenges himself on us for having invaded his domain."

Nell was allowed to hear as little as possible of these discussions. Indeed, she showed no desire to enter into them, although it was very evident that she shared in the anxieties of her adopted parents. The melancholy in her countenance bore witness to much mental agitation.

It was at length resolved that James Starr, together with Simon and Harry, should return to the scene of the disaster, and endeavor to satisfy themselves as to the cause of it. They mentioned their project to no one. To those unacquainted with the group of facts on which it was based, the opinion of Starr and his friends could not fail to appear wholly inadmissible.

A few days later, the three friends proceeded in a small boat to examine the natural pillars on which had rested the solid earth forming the basin of Loch Katrine. They discovered that they had been right in suspecting that the massive columns had been undermined by blasting. The blackened traces of explosion were to be seen, the waters having subsided below the level of these mysterious operations Thus the fall of a portion of the vast vaulted dome was proved to have been premeditated by man, and by man's hand had it been effected.

"It is impossible to doubt it," said James Starr; "and who can say what might not have happened had the sea, instead of a little loch, been let in upon us?"

"You may well say that," cried the old overman, with a feeling of pride in his beloved mine; "for nothing less than a sea would have drowned our Aberfoyle. But, once more, what possible interest could any human being have in the destruction of our works?"

"It is quite incomprehensible," replied James Starr. "This case is something perfectly unlike that of a band of common criminals, who, concealing themselves in dens and caves, go forth to rob and pillage the surrounding country. The evil deeds of such men would certainly, in the course of three years have betrayed their existence and lurking-places. Neither can it be, as I sometimes used to think, that smugglers or coiners carried on their illegal practices in some distant and unknown corner of these prodigious caverns, and were consequently anxious to drive us out of them. But no one coins false money or obtains contraband goods only to conceal them!

"Yet it is clear that an implacable enemy has sworn the ruin of New Aberfoyle, and that some interest urges him to seek in every possible way to wreak his hatred upon us. He appears to be too weak to act openly, and lays his schemes in secret; but displays such intelligence as to render him a most formidable foe.

"My friends, he must understand better than we do the secrets of our domain, since he has all this time eluded our vigilance. He must be a man experienced in mining, skilled beyond the most skillful—that's certain, Simon! We have proof enough of that.

"Let me see! Have you never had a personal enemy, to whom your suspicions might point? Think well! There is such a thing as hatred which time never softens. Go back to recollections of your earliest days. What befalls us appears the work of a stern and patient will, and to explain it demands every effort of thought and memory."

Simon did not answer immediately—his mind evidently engaged in a close and candid survey of his past life. Presently, raising his head, "No," said he; "no! Heaven be my witness, neither Madge nor I have ever injured anybody. We cannot believe that we have a single enemy in the world."

"Ah! if Nell would only speak!" cried the engineer.

"Mr. Starr—and you, father," said Harry, "I do beg of you to keep silence on this matter, and not to question my poor Nell. I know she is very anxious and uneasy; and I feel positive that some great secret painfully oppresses her heart. Either she knows nothing it would be of any use for us to hear, or she considers it her duty to be silent. It is impossible to doubt her affection for us—for all of us. If at a future time she informs me of what she has hitherto concealed from us, you shall know about it immediately."

"So be it, then, Harry," answered the engineer; "and yet I must say Nell's silence, if she knows anything, is to me perfectly inexplicable."

Harry would have continued her defense; but the engineer stopped him, saying, "All right, Harry; we promise to say no more about it to your future wife."

"With my father's consent she shall be my wife without further delay."

"My boy," said old Simon, "your marriage shall take place this very day month. Mr. Starr, will you undertake the part of Nell's father?"

"You may reckon upon me for that, Simon," answered the engineer.

They then returned to the cottage, but said not a word of the result of their examinations in the mine, so that to the rest of its inhabitants, the bursting in of the vaulted roof of the caverns continued to be regarded as a mere accident. There was but a loch the less in Scotland.

Nell gradually resumed her customary duties, and Harry made good use of her little visit to the upper air, in the instructions he gave her. She enjoyed the recollections of life above ground, yet without regretting it. The somber region she had loved as a child, and in which her wedded life would be spent, was as dear to her as ever.

The approaching marriage created great excitement in New Aberfoyle. Good wishes poured in on all sides, and foremost among them were Jack Ryan's. He was detected busily practicing his best songs in preparation for the great day, which was to be celebrated by the whole population of Coal Town.

During the month preceding the wedding-day, there were more accidents occurring in New Aberfoyle than had ever been known in the place. One would have thought the approaching union of Harry and Nell actually provoked one catastrophe after another. These misfortunes happened chiefly at the further and lowest extremity of the works, and the cause of them was always in some way mysterious.

Thus, for instance, the wood-work of a distant gallery was discovered to be in flames, which were extinguished by Harry and his companions at the risk of their lives, by employing engines filled with water and carbonic acid, always kept ready in case of necessity. The lamp used by the incendiary was found; but no clew whatever as to who he could be.

Another time an inundation took place in consequence of the stanchions of a water-tank giving way; and Mr. Starr ascertained beyond a doubt that these supports had first of all been partially sawn through. Harry, who had been overseeing the works near the place at the time, was buried in the falling rubbish, and narrowly escaped death.

A few days afterwards, on the steam tramway, a train of trucks, which Harry was passing along, met with an obstacle on the rails, and was overturned. It was then discovered that a beam had been laid across the line. In short, events of this description became so numerous that the miners were seized with a kind of panic, and it required all the influence of their chiefs to keep them on the works.

"You would think that there was a whole band of these ruffians," Simon kept saying, "and we can't lay hands on a single one of them."

Search was made in all directions. The county police were on the alert night and day, yet discovered nothing. The evil intentions seeming specially designed to injure Harry. Starr forbade him to venture alone beyond the ordinary limits of the works.

They were equally careful of Nell, although, at Harry's entreaty, these malicious attempts to do harm were concealed from her, because they might remind her painfully of former times. Simon and Madge watched over her by day and by night with a sort of stern solicitude. The poor child yielded to their wishes, without a remark or a complaint.

Did she perceive that they acted with a view to her interest? Probably she did. And on her part, she seemed to watch over others, and was never easy unless all whom she loved were together in the cottage.

When Harry came home in the evening, she could not restrain expressions of child-like joy, very unlike her usual manner, which was rather reserved than demonstrative. As soon as day broke, she was astir before anyone else, and her constant uneasiness lasted all day until the hour of return home from work.

Harry became very anxious that their marriage should take place. He thought that, when the irrevocable step was taken, malevolence would be disarmed, and that Nell would never feel safe until she was his wife. James Starr, Simon, and Madge, were all of the same opinion, and everyone counted the intervening days, for everyone suffered from the most uncomfortable forebodings.

It was perfectly evident that nothing relating to Nell was indifferent to this hidden foe, whom it was impossible to meet or to avoid. Therefore it seemed quite possible that the solemn act of her marriage with Harry might be the occasion of some new and dreadful outbreak of his hatred.

One morning, a week before the day appointed for the ceremony, Nell, rising early, went out of the cottage before anyone else. No sooner had she crossed the threshold than a cry of indescribable anguish escaped her lips.

Her voice was heard throughout the dwelling; in a moment, Madge, Harry, and Simon were at her side. Nell was pale as death, her countenance agitated, her features expressing the utmost horror. Unable to speak, her eyes were riveted on the door of the cottage, which she had just opened.

With rigid fingers she pointed to the following words traced upon it during the night: "Simon Ford, you have robbed me of the last vein in our old pit. Harry, your son, has robbed me of Nell. Woe betide you! Woe betide you all! Woe betide New Aberfoyle!—SILFAX."

"Silfax!" exclaimed Simon and Madge together.

"Who is this man?" demanded Harry, looking alternately at his father and at the maiden.

"Silfax!" repeated Nell in tones of despair, "Silfax!"—and, murmuring this name, her whole frame shuddering with fear and agitation, she was borne away to her chamber by old Madge.

James Starr, hastening to the spot, read the threatening sentences again and again.

"The hand which traced these lines," said he at length, "is the same which wrote me the letter contradicting yours, Simon. The man calls himself Silfax. I see by your troubled manner that you know him. Who is this Silfax?"

***

## CHAPTER XVII

## THE "MONK"

This name revealed everything to the old overman. It was that of the last "monk" of the Dochart pit.

In former days, before the invention of the safety-lamp, Simon had known this fierce man, whose business it was to go daily, at the risk of his life, to produce partial explosions of fire-damp in the passages. He used to see this strange solitary being, prowling about the mine, always accompanied by a monstrous owl, which he called Harfang, who assisted him in his perilous occupation, by soaring with a lighted match to places Silfax was unable to reach.

One day this old man disappeared, and at the same time also, a little orphan girl born in the mine, who had no relation but himself, her great-grandfather. It was perfectly evident now that this child was Nell. During the fifteen years, up to the time when she was saved by Harry, they must have lived in some secret abyss of the mine.

The old overman, full of mingled compassion and anger, made known to the engineer and Harry all that the name of Silfax had revealed to him. It explained the whole mystery. Silfax was the mysterious being so long vainly sought for in the depths of New Aberfoyle.

"So you knew him, Simon?" demanded Mr. Starr.

"Yes, that I did," replied the overman. "The Harfang man, we used to call him. Why, he was old then! He must be fifteen or twenty years older than I am. A wild, savage sort of fellow, who held aloof from everyone and was known to fear nothing—neither fire nor water. It was his own fancy to follow the trade of 'monk,' which few would have liked. The constant danger of the business had unsettled his brain. He was prodigiously strong, and he knew the mine as no one else—at any rate, as well as I did. He lived on a small allowance. In faith, I believed him dead years ago."

"But," resumed James Starr, "what does he mean by those words, 'You have robbed me of the last vein of our old mine'?"

"Ah! there it is," replied Simon; "for a long time it had been a fancy of his—I told you his mind was deranged—that he had a right to the mine of Aberfoyle; so he became more and more savage in temper the deeper the Dochart pit—his pit!—was worked out. It just seemed as if it was his own body that suffered from every blow of the pickax. You must remember that, Madge?"

"Ay, that I do, Simon," replied she.

"I can recollect all this," resumed Simon, "since I have seen the name of Silfax on the door. But I tell you, I thought the man was dead, and never imagined that the spiteful being we have so long sought for could be the old fireman of the Dochart pit."

"Well, now, then," said Starr, "it is all quite plain. Chance made known to Silfax the new vein of coal. With the egotism of madness, he believed himself the owner of a treasure he must conceal and defend. Living in the mine, and wandering about day and night, he perceived that you had discovered the secret, and had written in all haste to beg me to come. Hence the letter contradicting yours; hence, after my arrival, all the accidents that occurred, such as the block of stone thrown at Harry, the broken ladder at the Yarrow shaft, the obstruction of the openings into the wall of the new cutting; hence, in short, our imprisonment, and then our deliverance, brought about by the kind assistance of Nell, who acted of course without the knowledge of this man Silfax, and contrary to his intentions."

"You describe everything exactly as it must have happened, Mr. Starr," returned old Simon. "The old 'Monk' is mad enough now, at any rate!"

"All the better," quoth Madge.

"I don't know that," said Starr, shaking his head; "it is a terrible sort of madness this."

"Ah! now I understand that the very thought of him must have terrified poor little Nell, and also I see that she could not bear to denounce her grandfather. What a miserable time she must have had of it with the old man!"

"Miserable with a vengeance," replied Simon, "between that savage and his owl, as savage as himself. Depend upon it, that bird isn't dead. That was what put our lamp out, and also so nearly cut the rope by which Harry and Nell were suspended."

"And then, you see," said Madge, "this news of the marriage of our son with his granddaughter added to his rancor and ill-will."

"To be sure," said Simon. "To think that his Nell should marry one of the robbers of his own coal mine would just drive him wild altogether."

"He will have to make up his mind to it, however," cried Harry. "Mad as he is, we shall manage to convince him that Nell is better off with us here than ever she was in the caverns of the pit. I am sure, Mr. Starr, if we could only catch him, we should be able to make him listen to reason."

"My poor Harry! there is no reasoning with a madman," replied the engineer. "Of course it is better to know your enemy than not; but you must not fancy all is right because we have found out who he is. We must be on our guard, my friends; and to begin with, Harry, you positively must question Nell. She will perceive that her silence is no longer reasonable. Even for her grandfather's own interest, she ought to speak now. For his own sake, as well as for ours, these insane plots must be put a stop to."

"I feel sure, Mr. Starr," answered Harry, "that Nell will of herself propose to tell you what she knows. You see it was from a sense of duty that she has been silent hitherto. My mother was very right to take her to her room just now. She much needed time to recover her spirits; but now I will go for her."

"You need not do so, Harry," said the maiden in a clear and firm voice, as she entered at that moment the room in which they were. Nell was very pale; traces of tears were in her eyes; but her whole manner showed that she had nerved herself to act as her loyal heart dictated as her duty.

"Nell!" cried Harry, springing towards her.

The girl arrested her lover by a gesture, and continued, "Your father and mother, and you, Harry, must now know all. And you too, Mr. Starr, must remain ignorant of nothing that concerns the child you have received, and whom Harry—unfortunately for him, alas!—drew from the abyss."

"Oh, Nell! what are you saying?" cried Harry.

"Allow her to speak," said James Starr in a decided tone.

"I am the granddaughter of old Silfax," resumed Nell. "I never knew a mother till the day I came here," added she, looking at Madge.

"Blessed be that day, my daughter!" said the old woman.

"I knew no father till I saw Simon Ford," continued Nell; "nor friend till the day when Harry's hand touched mine. Alone with my grandfather I have lived during fifteen years in the remote and most solitary depths of the mine. I say ***with*** my grandfather, but I can scarcely use the expression, for I seldom saw him. When he disappeared from Old Aberfoyle, he concealed himself in caverns known only to himself. In his way he was kind to me, dreadful as he was; he fed me with whatever he could procure from outside the mine; but I can dimly recollect that in my earliest years I was the nursling of a goat, the death of which was a bitter grief to me. My grandfather, seeing my distress, brought me another animal—a dog he said it was. But, unluckily, this dog was lively, and barked. Grandfather did not like anything cheerful. He had a horror of noise, and had taught me to be silent; the dog he could not teach to be quiet, so the poor animal very soon disappeared. My grandfather's companion was a ferocious bird, Harfang, of which, at first, I had a perfect horror; but this creature, in spite of my dislike to it, took such a strong affection for me, that I could not help returning it. It even obeyed me better than its master, which used to make me quite uneasy, for my grandfather was jealous. Harfang and I did not dare to let him see us much together; we both knew it would be dangerous. But I am talking too much about myself: the great thing is about you."

"No, my child," said James Starr, "tell us everything that comes to your mind."

"My grandfather," continued Nell, "always regarded your abode in the mine with a very evil eye—not that there was any lack of space. His chosen refuge was far—very far from you. But he could not bear to feel that you were there. If I asked any questions about the people up above us, his face grew dark, he gave no answer, and continued quite silent for a long time afterwards. But when he perceived that, not content with the old domain, you seemed to think of encroaching upon his, then indeed his anger burst forth. He swore that, were you to succeed in reaching the new mine, you should assuredly perish. Notwithstanding his great age, his strength is astonishing, and his threats used to make me tremble."

"Go on, Nell, my child," said Simon to the girl, who paused as though to collect her thoughts.

"On the occasion of your first attempt," resumed Nell, "as soon as my grandfather saw that you were fairly inside the gallery leading to New Aberfoyle, he stopped up the opening, and turned it into a prison for you. I only knew you as shadows dimly seen in the gloom of the pit, but I could not endure the idea that you would die of hunger in these horrid places; and so, at the risk of being detected, I succeeded in obtaining bread and water for you during some days. I should have liked to help you to escape, but it was so difficult to avoid the vigilance of my grandfather. You were about to die. Then arrived Jack Ryan and the others. By the providence of God I met with them, and instantly guided them to where you were. When my grandfather discovered what I had done, his rage against me was terrible. I expected death at his hands. After that my life became insupportable to me. My grandfather completely lost his senses.

He proclaimed himself King of Darkness and Flame; and when he heard your tools at work on coal-beds which he considered entirely his own, he became furious and beat me cruelly. I would have fled from him, but it was impossible, so narrowly did he watch me. At last, in a fit of ungovernable fury, he threw me down into the abyss where you found me, and disappeared, vainly calling on Harfang, which faithfully stayed by me, to follow him. I know not how long I remained there, but I felt I was at the point of death when you, my Harry, came and saved me. But now you all see that the grandchild of old Silfax can never be the wife of Harry Ford, because it would be certain death to you all!"

"Nell!" cried Harry.

"No," continued the maiden, "my resolution is taken. By one means only can your ruin be averted; I must return to my grandfather. He threatens to destroy the whole of New Aberfoyle. His is a soul incapable of mercy or forgiveness, and no mortal can say to what horrid deed the spirit of revenge will lead him. My duty is clear; I should be the most despicable creature on earth did I hesitate to perform it. Farewell! I thank you all heartily. You only have taught me what happiness is. Whatever may befall, believe that my whole heart remains with you."

At these words, Simon, Madge, and Harry started up in an agony of grief, exclaiming in tones of despair, "What, Nell! is it possible you would leave us?"

James Starr put them all aside with an air of authority, and, going straight up to Nell, he took both her hands in his, saying quietly, "Very right, my child; you have said exactly what you ought to say; and now listen to what we have to say in reply. We shall not let you go away; if necessary, we shall keep you by force. Do you think we could be so base as to accept of your generous proposal? These threats of Silfax are formidable—no doubt about it! But, after all, a man is but a man, and we can take precautions. You will tell us, will you not, even for his own sake, all you can about his habits and his lurking-places? All we want to do is to put it out of his power to do harm, and perhaps bring him to reason."

"You want to do what is quite impossible," said Nell. "My grandfather is everywhere and nowhere. I have never seen his retreats. I have never seen him sleep. If he meant to conceal himself, he used to leave me alone, and vanish. When I took my resolution, Mr. Starr, I was aware of everything you could say against it. Believe me, there is but one way to render Silfax powerless, and that will be by my return to him. Invisible himself, he secs everything that goes on. Just think whether it is likely he could discover your very thoughts and intentions, from that time when the letter was written to Mr. Starr, up to now that my marriage with Harry has been arranged, if he did not possess the extraordinary faculty of knowing everything. As far as I am able to judge, my grandfather, in his very insanity, is a man of most powerful mind. He formerly used to talk to me on very lofty subjects. He taught me the existence of God, and never deceived me but on one point, which was—that he made me believe that all men were base and perfidious, because he wished to inspire me with his own hatred of all the human race. When Harry brought me to the cottage, you thought I was simply ignorant of mankind, but, far beyond that, I was in mortal fear of you all. Ah, forgive me! I assure you, for many days I believed myself in the power of wicked wretches, and I longed to escape. You, Madge, first led me to perceive the truth, not by anything you said, but by the sight of your daily life, for I saw that your husband and son loved and respected you! Then all these good and happy workmen, who so revere and trust Mr. Starr, I used to think they were slaves; and when, for the first time, I saw the whole population of Aberfoyle come to church and kneel down to pray to God, and praise Him for His infinite goodness, I said to myself, 'My grandfather has deceived me.' But now, enlightened by all you have taught me, I am inclined to think he himself is deceived. I mean to return to the secret passages I formerly frequented with him. He is certain to be on the watch. I will call to him; he will hear me, and who knows but that, by returning to him, I may be able to bring him to the knowledge of the truth?"

The maiden spoke without interruption, for all felt that it was good for her to open her whole heart to her friends.

But when, exhausted by emotion, and with eyes full of tears, she ceased speaking, Harry turned to old Madge and said, "Mother, what should you think of the man who could forsake the noble girl whose words you have been listening to?"

"I should think he was a base coward," said Madge, "and, were he my son, I should renounce and curse him."

"Nell, do you hear what our mother says?" resumed Harry. "Wherever you go I will follow you. If you persist in leaving us, we will go away together."

"Harry! Harry!" cried Nell.

Overcome by her feelings, the girl's lips blanched, and she sank into the arms of Madge, who begged she might be left alone with her.

***

## CHAPTER XVIII

## NELL'S WEDDING

It was agreed that the inhabitants of the cottage must keep more on their guard than ever. The threats of old Silfax were too serious to be disregarded. It was only too possible that he possessed some terrible means by which the whole of Aberfoyle might be annihilated.

Armed sentinels were posted at the various entrances to the mine, with orders to keep strict watch day and night. Any stranger entering the mine was brought before James Starr, that he might give an account of himself. There being no fear of treason among the inhabitants of Coal Town, the threatened danger to the subterranean colony was made known to them. Nell was informed of all the precautions taken, and became more tranquil, although she was not free from uneasiness. Harry's determination to follow her wherever she went compelled her to promise not to escape from her friends.

During the week preceding the wedding, no accident whatever occurred in Aberfoyle. The system of watching was carefully maintained, but the miners began to recover from the panic, which had seriously interrupted the work of excavation. James Starr continued to look out for Silfax. The old man having vindictively declared that Nell should never marry Simon's son, it was natural to suppose that he would not hesitate to commit any violent deed which would hinder their union.

The examination of the mine was carried on minutely. Every passage and gallery was searched, up to those higher ranges which opened out among the ruins of Dundonald Castle. It was rightly supposed that through this old building Silfax passed out to obtain what was needful for the support of his miserable existence (which he must have done, either by purchasing or thieving).

As to the "fire-maidens," James Starr began to think that appearance must have been produced by some jet of fire-damp gas which, issuing from that part of the pit, could be lighted by Silfax. He was not far wrong; but all search for proof of this was fruitless, and the continued strain of anxiety in this perpetual effort to detect a malignant and invisible being rendered the engineer—outwardly calm—an unhappy man.

As the wedding-day approached, his dread of some catastrophe increased, and he could not but speak of it to the old overman, whose uneasiness soon more than equaled his own. At length the day came. Silfax had given no token of existence.

By daybreak the entire population of Coal Town was astir. Work was suspended; overseers and workmen alike desired to do honor to Simon Ford and his son. They all felt they owed a large debt of gratitude to these bold and persevering men, by whose means the mine had been restored to its former prosperity. The ceremony was to take place at eleven o'clock, in St. Giles's chapel, which stood on the shores of Loch Malcolm.

At the appointed time, Harry left the cottage, supporting his mother on his arm, while Simon led the bride. Following them came Starr, the engineer, composed in manner, but in reality nerved to expect the worst, and Jack Ryan, stepping superb in full Highland piper's costume. Then came the other mining engineers, the principal people of Coal Town, the friends and comrades of the old overman—every member of this great family of miners forming the population of New Aberfoyle.

In the outer world, the day was one of the hottest of the month of August, peculiarly oppressive in northern countries. The sultry air penetrated the depths of the coal mine, and elevated the temperature. The air which entered through the ventilating shafts, and the great tunnel of Loch Malcolm, was charged with electricity, and the barometer, it was afterwards remarked, had fallen in a remarkable manner. There was, indeed, every indication that a storm might burst forth beneath the rocky vault which formed the roof of the enormous crypt of the very mine itself.

But the inhabitants were not at that moment troubling themselves about the chances of atmospheric disturbance above ground. Everybody, as a matter of course, had put on his best clothes for the occasion. Madge was dressed in the fashion of days gone by, wearing the "toy" and the "rokelay," or Tartan plaid, of matrons of the olden time, old Simon wore a coat of which Bailie Nicol Jarvie himself would have approved.

Nell had resolved to show nothing of her mental agitation; she forbade her heart to beat, or her inward terrors to betray themselves, and the brave girl appeared before all with a calm and collected aspect. She had declined every ornament of dress, and the very simplicity of her attire added to the charming elegance of her appearance. Her hair was bound with the "snood," the usual head-dress of Scottish maidens.

All proceeded towards St. Giles's chapel, which had been handsomely decorated for the occasion.

The electric discs of light which illuminated Coal Town blazed like so many suns. A luminous atmosphere pervaded New Aberfoyle. In the chapel, electric lamps shed a glow over the stained-glass windows, which shone like fiery kaleidoscopes. At the porch of the chapel the minister awaited the arrival of the wedding party.

It approached, after having passed in stately procession along the shore of Loch Malcolm. Then the tones of the organ were heard, and, preceded by the minister, the group advanced into the chapel. The Divine blessing was first invoked on all present. Then Harry and Nell remained alone before the minister, who, holding the sacred book in his hand, proceeded to say, "Harry, will you take Nell to be your wife, and will you promise to love her always?"

"I promise," answered the young man in a firm and steady voice.

"And you, Nell," continued the minister, "will you take Harry to be your husband, and—"

Before he could finish the sentence, a prodigious noise resounded from without. One of the enormous rocks, on which was formed the terrace overhanging the banks of Loch Malcolm, had suddenly given way and opened without explosion, disclosing a profound abyss, into which the waters were now wildly plunging.

In another instant, among the shattered rocks and rushing waves appeared a canoe, which a vigorous arm propelled along the surface of the lake. In the canoe was seen the figure of an old man standing upright. He was clothed in a dark mantle, his hair was dishevelled, a long white beard fell over his breast, and in his hand he bore a lighted Davy safety lamp, the flame being protected by the metallic gauze of the apparatus.

In a loud voice this old man shouted, "The fire-damp is upon you! Woe—woe betide ye all!"

At the same moment the slight smell peculiar to carburetted hydrogen was perceptibly diffused through the atmosphere. And, in truth, the fall of the rock had made a passage of escape for an enormous quantity of explosive gas, accumulated in vast cavities, the openings to which had hitherto been blocked up.

Jets and streams of the fire-damp now rose upward in the vaulted dome; and well did that fierce old man know that the consequence of what he had done would be to render explosive the whole atmosphere of the mine.

James Starr and several others, having hastily quitted the chapel, and perceived the imminence of the danger, now rushed back, crying out in accents of the utmost alarm, "Fly from the mine! Fly instantly from the mine!"

"Now for the fire-damp! Here comes the fire-damp!" yelled the old man, urging his canoe further along the lake.

Harry with his bride, his father and his mother, left the chapel in haste and in terror.

"Fly! fly for your lives!" repeated James Starr. Alas! it was too late to fly! Old Silfax stood there, prepared to fulfill his last dreadful threat—prepared to stop the marriage of Nell and Harry by overwhelming the entire population of the place beneath the ruins of the coal mine.

As he stood ready to accomplish this act of vengeance, his enormous owl, whose white plumage was marked with black spots, was seen hovering directly above his head.

At that moment a man flung himself into the waters of the lake, and swam vigorously towards the canoe.

It was Jack Ryan, fully determined to reach the madman before he could do the dreadful deed of destruction.

Silfax saw him coming. Instantly he smashed the glass of his lamp, and, snatching out the burning wick, waved it in the air.

Silence like death fell upon the astounded multitude. James Starr, in the calmness of despair, marvelled that the inevitable explosion was even for a moment delayed.

Silfax, gazing upwards with wild and contracted features, appeared to become aware that the gas, lighter than the lower atmosphere, was accumulating far up under the dome; and at a sign from him the owl, seizing in its claw the lighted match, soared upwards to the vaulted roof, towards which the madman pointed with outstretched arm.

Another second and New Aberfoyle would be no more.

Suddenly Nell sprang from Harry's arms, and, with a bright look of inspiration, she ran to the very brink of the waters of the lake. "Harfang! Harfang!" cried she in a clear voice; "here! come to me!"

The faithful bird, surprised, appeared to hesitate in its flight. Presently, recognizing Nell's voice, it dropped the burning match into the water, and, describing a wide circle, flew downwards, alighting at the maiden's feet.

Then a terrible cry echoed through the vaulted roofs. It was the last sound uttered by old Silfax.

Just as Jack Ryan laid his hand on the edge of the canoe, the old man, foiled in his purpose of revenge, cast himself headlong into the waters of the lake.

"Save him! oh, save him!" shrieked Nell in a voice of agony. Immediately Harry plunged into the water, and, swimming towards Jack Ryan, he dived repeatedly.

But his efforts were useless. The waters of Loch Malcolm yielded not their prey: they closed forever over Silfax.

***

## CHAPTER XIX

## THE LEGEND OF OLD SILFAX

Six months after these events, the marriage, so strangely interrupted, was finally celebrated in St. Giles's chapel, and the young couple, who still wore mourning garments, returned to the cottage. James Starr and Simon Ford, henceforth free from the anxieties which had so long distressed them, joyously presided over the entertainment which followed the ceremony, and prolonged it to the following day.

On this memorable occasion, Jack Ryan, in his favorite character of piper, and in all the glory of full dress, blew up his chanter, and astonished the company by the unheard of achievement of playing, singing, and dancing all at once.

It is needless to say that Harry and Nell were happy. These loving hearts, after the trials they had gone through found in their union the happiness they deserved.

As to Simon Ford, the ex-overman of New Aberfoyle, he began to talk of celebrating his golden wedding, after fifty years of marriage with good old Madge, who liked the idea immensely herself.

"And after that, why not golden wedding number two?"

"You would like a couple of fifties, would you, Mr. Simon?" said Jack Ryan.

"All right, my boy," replied the overman quietly, "I see nothing against it in this fine climate of ours, and living far from the luxury and intemperance of the outer world."

Will the dwellers in Coal Town ever be called to witness this second ceremony? Time will show. Certainly the strange bird of old Silfax seemed destined to attain a wonderful longevity. The Harfang continued to haunt the gloomy recesses of the cave. After the old man's death, Nell had attempted to keep the owl, but in a very few days he flew away. He evidently disliked human society as much as his master had done, and, besides that, he appeared to have a particular spite against Harry. The jealous bird seemed to remember and hate him for having carried off Nell from the deep abyss, notwithstanding all he could do to prevent him. Still, at long intervals, Nell would see the creature hovering above Loch Malcolm.

Could he possibly be watching for his friend of yore? Did he strive to pierce, with keen eye, the depths which had engulfed his master?

The history of the Harfang became legendary, and furnished Jack Ryan with many a tale and song. Thanks to him, the story of old Silfax and his bird will long be preserved, and handed down to future generations of the Scottish peasantry.

**The End.**